# C∞kies for Santa

## Volume 1

## Lisa Oakman

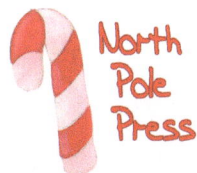

North Pole Press

This book belongs to:

．．．．．．．．．．．．．．．．．．．．．．．．．．．．．．．．．．．．．．．．．．．．．．．．．．．．．．．．．．．．．

*This book is dedicated to my four wonderful children: Adelaide, Idela, Cole & Morgan. May you always brighten the world with your smiles. I love you.*

*- Lisa*

ISBN-10: 0615597076
ISBN-13: 978-0615597072

North Pole Press takes pride in the celebration of the Christmas season, as well as in the holiday books in which we release. We welcome your comments and suggestions. You can also learn more about this book by visiting our website, http://www.northpolepress.com .

First US Edition Published 2013

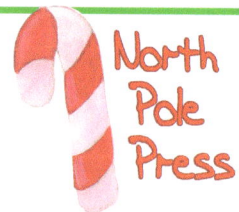

North Pole Press

# Contents

Dear Children,

     It's that wonderful time of year again, when all of us here at the North Pole are busy gearing up for the long journey that will take me to all of your homes come Christmas Eve. I'm so excited! But, most of all, I can't wait to see what cookies await me! Yummy goodness!

     Over the years, children often write to me, asking what my favorite cookies are. Honestly, I don't have a favorite cookie, as I love all types of cookies from all over the world. However, these letters gave me an idea... an idea to share all of these different cookies with you, so that you too can enjoy the many cookies I find all over the world.

     So, I devised this cookbook. Oh, and don't worry, when you've finished enjoying all of the cookies in this cookbook, I will have eleven more cookie cookbooks to follow! I told you I love all types of cookies!

     Also, in this cookbook you'll hear from the "Mrs.", who will be adding her two cents with healthy ingredient substitution alternatives. You'll also hear from Rudolph, which many of you know as my main lead reindeer. He'll help guide you to the part of the world in which I typically find certain cookies on Christmas Eve, and Avalanche, my main lead sled dog (slash comedian-extraordinaire, who is always chewing on a funny bone). She'll break down the top secret language of the North Pole for you. Betcha didn't know dog sledding was a hobby of mine!?!

     Well, enjoy your cookie making (and eating - I know I can't wait to eat them too) and don't forget to be safe while working in the kitchen and to help clean up after you're done!

     Merry Christmas to all of you!

All my love,

*Santa*

# Healthy Substituti🍪ns

My Dear Ones,

Did you know that each Christmas Eve Santa devours well over a million cookies? Can you imagine? That's a whole lot of cookies!

So, to help keep Santa healthy, as well as you and your family, I've included a list of healthy substitutions for you to use, if you choose.

Also, on the following page you'll find a list of regular substitutions should you find that you are missing an ingredient or two and need something in a pinch.

Stay healthy and happy cookie making!

Love,
*Mrs. Claus*

## Sugar Substitutions:

- substitute each cup of **sugar** with 2/3 cup of **agave nectar** and reduce any liquid in the recipe by 1/4 cup
- substitute each cup of **sugar** with an equal amount of **brown rice malt syrup** and reduce any liquid in the recipe by 1/4 cup, for each cup of brown rice malt syrup used
- substitute each cup of **sugar** with 3/4 cup of **fruit juice** (such as apple juice concentrate, orange juice concentrate or white grapefruit concentrate, etc.), but you must also reduce any liquid in the recipe by 3 tablespoons
- you can also substitute **sugar** with **stevia liquid** or **stevia powder**, follow the substitution instructions provided by the manufacturer, results may vary

## Other Substitutions:

- 1 square of **baking chocolate** - substitute with 3 tablespoons of **cocoa** and 1 tablespoon of **butter**, or 3 tablespoons of **carob** and 2 tablespoons of **water**
- 1 teaspoon of **baking powder** - substitute with 1/2 teaspoon of **cream of tartar** and 1/2 teaspoon of **baking powder**
- **butter** - substitute with an equal amount of **margarine**, **applesauce** or **fruit puree** (like prune)
- **cream cheese** - substitute with an equal amount of **yogurt cheese**
- **shortening** - substitute with an equal amount of **olive**, **safflower**, **corn**, **sunflower**, **canola** or **soybean oil**
- **vegetable oil** - substitute with an equal amount of **canola** or **soybean oil**
- **whole milk** - substitute with an equal amount of **low-fat** or **skim milk**
  - **whole egg** - substitute with **two egg whites** or 1/4 cup **egg substitute**

*4*

# Regular Substituti⬤ns

## Sugar Substitutions:

- substitute each cup of **sugar** with an equal amount of **brown sugar**, packed
- substitute each cup of **sugar** with 3/4 cup of **maple syrup**
- substitute each cup of **sugar** with 3/4 cup of **honey**
- you can substitute up to one half of the **sugar** needed with **corn syrup**, but you'll also need to reduce any liquid in the recipe by 1/4 cup for each cup of syrup used (for example, 2 cups of sugar = 1 cup sugar, 1 cup corn syrup and a reduction of 1/4 cup of any liquid in the recipe)
- substitute each cup of **sugar** with 1 1/4 cups of **molasses**
- you can also substitute **sugar** with **artificial sweeteners**, follow the substitution instructions provided by the manufacturer, results may vary

## Spice Substitutions:

- **allspice** - substitute with an equal amount of **cinnamon** or **cassia**, or use only a dash of **nutmeg**, **mace** or **cloves**
- **anise seed** - substitute with an equal amount of **fennel seed**, **caraway seed** or with a few drops of **anise extract**
- **cinnamon** - substitute with **nutmeg** or **allspice**, for only 1/4 of the amount of cinnamon needed
- **cloves** - substitute with an equal amount of **allspice**, **cinnamon** or **nutmeg**
- **ginger** - substitute with an equal amount of **allspice**, **cinnamon**, **nutmeg** or **mace**
- **nutmeg** - substitute with an equal amount of **cinnamon**, **ginger** or **mace**

## Other Substitutions:

- **almond extract** - substitute with an equal amount of **amaretto**
- **brown sugar** - substitute each cup of brown sugar with a cup of **sugar** plus two tablespoons of **molasses**
- **cream cheese** - substitute with an equal amount of **neufchatel cheese**
- **crème de menthe** - substitute with an equal amount of **spearmint extract**
- **milk** - substitute each cup of milk with a 1/2 cup of **water** and a 1/2 cup of **evaporated milk**

*5*

# Where in the World?

By: Rudolph

Hi kids!

    As you know I have one of the best jobs in the world, traveling with Santa every Christmas Eve, to deliver gifts to all of you wonderfully good children! Which means that I get to see all sorts of different parts of the world! Isn't that cool?

    Throughout this cookbook, you'll see me holding different flags, which will show you what part of the country that Santa may find a certain cookie in. You will also see the county's name alongside the flag. So, when you make each cookie, be sure to look at what part of the world that cookie came from!

# Lingo of the North Pole

By: Avalanche

Hiya kiddos!

    Here at the North Pole, which is overrun by elves (if you ask me), we have a different way of speaking (again thanks to the elves). So, throughout the cookbook you'll find words that may vary slightly from your own language (unless, of course, you speak elven), in bold print.

    Here are the translations:

| | | |
|---|---|---|
| **lingo** ----> language | **mingle/d** ---> intermix | **fridge** ----> refridgerator |
| **mush** ---> mix well | **orb/s** --------> ball | **jimmies** -> sprinkles |
| **whirl** ----> blend | **squish** ------> flatten that bad boy! |

**6**

# Kitchen Preparation & Safety

**ALWAYS** *ask an adult to assist you.*

**ALWAYS** *wash & dry your hands before preparing any cookies.*

**ALWAYS** *pre-wash surfaces with hot soap and water prior to using it (like countertops or cutting boards).*

**ALWAYS** *pre-arrange the racks in the oven prior to turning it on.*

**ALWAYS** *wear potholders, on each hand, when putting anything in the oven, or when removing anything from the oven.*

**ALWAYS** *put hot objects on a heat proof surface or trivet.*

**ALWAYS** *pick knives up by the handle, never by the blade.*

**ALWAYS** *wipe your dirty hands on a towel or apron, never on your clothing.*

When cooking on a stovetop, **ALWAYS** make sure that all pan and pot handles are turned towards the center of the stovetop.

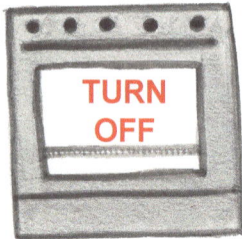

TURN OFF

**ALWAYS** make sure that the oven, stovetop and mixer are shut off after you are done using them.

**ALWAYS** wash and dry your hands after you have finished preparing the cookies.

**ALWAYS** help clean up when the baking is done. Note: it helps greatly if you clean up as you go

# Conversion Chart

| CUP | FLUID OZ. | TABLESPOONS | TEASPOONS | MILLILITER |
|---|---|---|---|---|
| 1 cup | 8 oz. | 16 tablespoons | 48 teaspoons | 237 ml |
| 3/4 cup | 6 oz. | 12 tablespoons | 36 teaspoons | 177 ml |
| 2/3 cup | 5 oz. | 11 tablespoons | 32 teaspoons | 158 ml |
| 1/2 cup | 4 oz. | 8 tablespoons | 24 teaspoons | 118 ml |
| 1/3 cup | 3 oz. | 5 tablespoons | 16 teaspoons | 79 ml |
| 1/4 cup | 2 oz. | 4 tablespoons | 12 teaspoons | 59 ml |
| 1/8 cup | 1 oz. | 2 tablespoons | 6 teaspoons | 30 ml |
| 1/16 cup | 1/2 oz. | 1 tablespoon | 3 teaspoons | 15 ml |

# Grocery List

## Alcohol Section
crème de menthe
brandy (normal, peach)

## Baking Section
active dry yeast
almond paste
almonds (ground, sliced, finely chopped)
anise seed (ground, whole)
baking powder
baking soda
bar of unsweetened baking chocolate
black walnuts  (chopped)
brown sugar (light, dark)
candied pineapple
candy canes or peppermint candies
chocolate chunks
cinnamon (ground, stick)
cloves (ground, whole)
cocoa (plain, dutch processed)
coconut (shredded)
corn syrup (light, dark)
cream of tartar
dried fruit
evaporated milk
extracts (vanilla, mexican vanilla, almond, maple, anise, peppermint, lemon)
flour (all-purpose, cake)
food coloring (red, green, yellow, blue)
ginger (ground)
golden raisins
green candied cherries
green colored sugar
hickory nuts (chopped)
honey
milk chocolate (bar, chips)
molasses
nutmeg (ground)
old fashioned oats
pecans (chopped, halves, whole)

pitted dates
red candied cherries
red colored sugar
salt
semisweet chocolate (bar, chips)
shortening (plain, butter flavored)
sprinkles
sugar (regular, superfine, confectioners')
sweetened condensed milk
toffee bits
vegetable oil
walnuts (chopped, finely chopped)
white chocolate chips
white pepper (ground)

## Condiment Section
fruit preserves
marshmallow fluff
peanut butter
vinegar
maraschino cherries

## Dairy Section
butter
buttermilk
cream cheese
eggs
lemon juice
light cream
milk
orange juice
whipping cream

## Fresh Fruit Section
lemons
oranges

## Specialty Section
vanilla bean

Note: list doesn't include substitution ingredients

# What Y🍪u'll Need:

**Mixing Bowls**

**Kitchen Spoon**

**Whisk**

**Parchment Paper**

PARCHMENT PAPER

**Wooden Spoon**

**Muffin Tin**
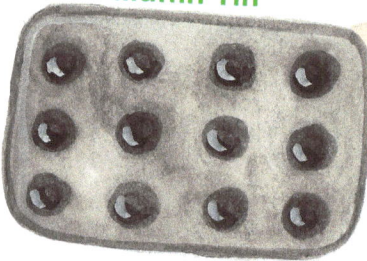

**Measuring Spoons**

**Pastry Brush**

**Metal Spatula**

**Pastry Bag**

**Wire Cooling Rack**

**Saucepans & Pots**

**Double Boiler**

**Rubber Spatula**

**Wax Paper**
WAX PAPER

**Rolling Pin**

**Kitchen Fork**

**Ice Cream Scoop**

Cookie Press

**Beater**

**8x8 baking pan**

Mason Jar

**Toothpicks**

**Glass**

**Plastic Wrap**

PLASTIC WRAP

Candy Thermometer

**Baking Sheets**

Speculaas Mold

**Kitchen Knife**

**Mixer with Mixing Bowl**

**Measuring Cup**

**Cookie Cutters**

*11*

# Ball Cookies

# Amish Gingers

## Directions:

Ready... set... now preheat that oven!

350° F

**1.** In a mixing bowl, **mush** the butter and sugar together. Next, add the egg, molasses, flour, ginger, cloves, cinnamon, and baking soda. **Whirl** until all of the ingredients have **mingled**.

**2.** Roll the dough into **orbs**, that are about an inch around. After they are in **orb** form roll each **orb** in the extra sugar.

**3.** Place the sugared **orbs** on an ungreased baking sheet. Carefully place the baking sheet in the oven and bake away.

7-9 minutes

**4.** When the time is up, cautiously remove the baking sheet from the oven and allow the cookies to sit on the baking sheet, placed on a heat proof surface, to cool for 5 minutes. After the 5 minutes is up remove the cookies from the baking sheet with a metal spatula and place them on a wire rack to cool off further.

## Ingredients:

3/4 cup butter, softened
1 cup sugar
1 egg
1/4 cup molasses
2 1/2 cups all-purpose flour
1 teaspoon ground ginger
1/2 teaspoon ground cloves
1 teaspoon ground cinnamon
1 1/2 teaspoon baking soda
extra sugar

## What you'll need:

measuring cups
measuring spoons
mixer with beater & bowl
baking sheet
metal spatula
wire cooling rack

# Cheesecake Chewies

## Ingredients:

1/2 cup butter, softened
1 (3 oz.) package cream cheese,
  softened
1 cup sugar
1 cup all-purpose flour
1/2 cup pecans, chopped

## What you'll need:

measuring cups
measuring spoons
mixer with beater & bowl
glass
baking sheet
metal spatula
wire cooling rack

## Directions:

Ready... set... now preheat that oven!

**375° F**

*1.* In a mixing bowl, **mush** the butter, cream cheese and sugar together. Next, add in the flour, and pecans. **Whirl** until all of the ingredients have **mingled**.

*2.* Roll the dough into **orbs**, that are about an inch around.

*3.* Place the **orbs** on an ungreased baking sheet and then use the bottom of a wet glass to gently **squish** each **orb** flat. Then carefully place the baking sheet in the oven and bake away.

**12-13 minutes**

*4.* When the time is up, cautiously remove the baking sheet from the oven and allow the cookies to sit on the baking sheet, placed on a heat proof surface, to cool for 5 minutes. After the 5 minutes is up remove the cookies from the baking sheet with a metal spatula and place them on a wire rack to cool off further.

# Chocolate Chewies

## Directions:

Ready... set... now preheat that oven!

**350° F**

*1.* In a saucepan melt the chocolate chips over low heat. Stir regularly with a wooden spoon until all of the chips have melted, then remove from heat.

*2.* In a mixing bowl, **mush** the butter and sugars together. Next, add in the eggs, melted chocolate and vanilla. Then slowly add in the flour, baking powder and baking soda. **Whirl** until all of the ingredients have **mingled**.

*3.* Roll the dough into **orbs**, that are about an inch around.

*4.* Place the **orbs** on a greased baking sheet. Carefully place the baking sheet in the oven and bake away.

**12-14 minutes**

*5.* When the time is up, cautiously remove the baking sheet from the oven and allow the cookies to sit on the baking sheet, placed on a heat proof surface, to cool for 5 minutes. After the 5 minutes is up remove the cookies from the baking sheet with a metal spatula and place them on a wire rack to cool off further.

## Ingredients:

2 cups milk chocolate chips
1 cup butter, softened
1 cup sugar
1 cup brown sugar, packed
4 eggs
1 teaspoon vanilla extract
4 cups all-purpose flour
1 teaspoon baking powder
1 teaspoon baking soda

## What you'll need:

measuring cups
measuring spoons
saucepan
wooden spoon
mixer with beater & bowl
baking sheet
metal spatula
wire cooling rack

# Fudge Balls

## Ingredients:

1 cup butter
3/4 cup brown sugar, packed
1 egg yolk
2 cups all-purpose flour
1/2 teaspoon salt
1/2 lb. fudge
   (see pg. 77 for recipe)

## What you'll need:

measuring cups
measuring spoons
mixer with beater & bowl
baking sheet
metal spatula
wire cooling rack

## Directions:

Ready... set... now preheat that oven!

**325° F**

*1.* In a mixing bowl, **mush** the butter and brown sugar together. Add the egg yolk, flour, and salt. **Whirl** until all of the ingredients have **mingled** into a dough. If needed you can chill the dough in the **fridge** until firm.

*2.* Roll the dough into **orbs**, that are about an inch around.

*3.* Place the **orbs** on an ungreased baking sheet and make an indentation in the middle of each ball with your thumb. Place a small piece of fudge in each indentation.

*4.* Carefully place the baking sheet in the oven and bake away.

**8-10 minutes**

*5.* When the time is up, cautiously remove the baking sheet from the oven and allow the cookies to sit on the baking sheet, placed on a heat proof surface, to cool for 5 minutes. After the 5 minutes is up remove the cookies from the baking sheet with a metal spatula and place them on a wire rack to cool off further.

United States of America

# Macaroons

## Directions:

Ready... set... now preheat that oven!

**350° F**

*1.* In a mixing bowl, **whirl** the coconut, extracts, salt and condensed milk together.

*2.* In a separate, small mixing bowl, beat the 2 egg whites until they reach stiff peaks. Once they have peaked, use a rubber spatula to fold the egg whites into the coconut mixture.

*3.* Roll the dough into **orbs**, that are about an inch around and place the **orbs** on a well greased baking sheet.

*4.* Carefully place the baking sheet in the oven and bake away.

**8-10 minutes**

*5.* When the time is up, cautiously remove the baking sheet from the oven and allow the cookies to sit on the baking sheet, placed on a heat proof surface, to cool for 3 minutes. After the 3 minutes is up remove the cookies from the baking sheet with a metal spatula and roll them in the confectioners sugar and place them on a wire rack to cool off further.

## Ingredients:

3 cups shredded coconut
1/2 teaspoon vanilla extract
1/2 teaspoon almond extract
1/8 teaspoon salt
2/3 cup sweetened condensed milk
2 egg whites
1 cup confectioners' sugar

## What you'll need:

measuring cups
measuring spoons
mixer with beater & bowl
small mixing bowl
rubber spatula
baking sheet
metal spatula
wire cooling rack

*France*

# Manteccaditos

## Ingredients:

3/4 cup butter
1/4 cup shortening
1 1/2 teaspoons almond extract
1/2 teaspoon vanilla extract
1/2 cup sugar
2 1/4 cups all-purpose flour
1/4 teaspoon ground nutmeg
5 maraschino cherries, cut into eighths

## What you'll need:

measuring cups
measuring spoons
mixer with beater & bowl
mixing bowl
kitchen spoon
baking sheet
metal spatula
wire cooling rack

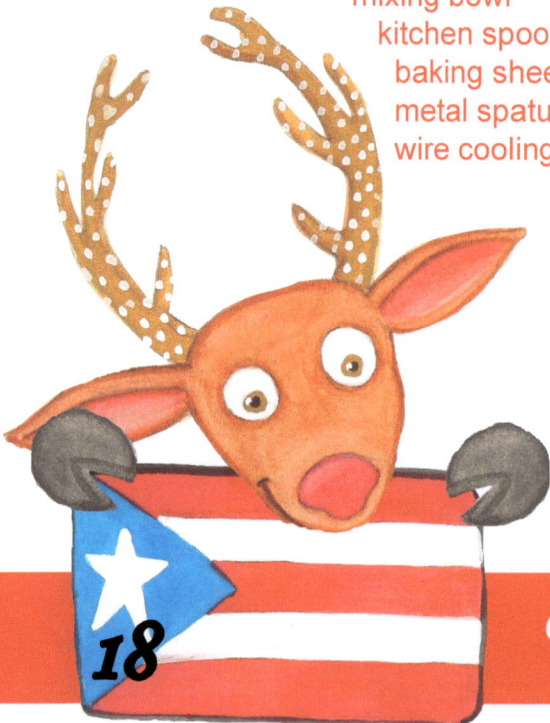

## Directions:

Ready... set... now preheat that oven!

**350° F**

*1.* In a mixing bowl, **mush** the butter, shortening, extracts and sugar together. Add the flour and nutmeg. **Whirl** until all of the ingredients have **mingled** into a dough.

*2.* Roll the dough into **orbs**, that are about an inch around.

*3.* Place the **orbs** on an ungreased baking sheet and use a wet cup bottom to gently **squish** each cookie flat. Then press a cherry piece in the middle of each cookie.

*4.* Carefully place the baking sheet in the oven and bake away.

**20 minutes**

*5.* When the time is up, cautiously remove the baking sheet from the oven and allow the cookies to sit on the baking sheet, placed on a heat proof surface, to cool for 5 minutes. After the 5 minutes is up remove the cookies from the baking sheet with a metal spatula and place them on a wire rack to cool off further.

*Puerto Rico*

# Snowballs

## Directions:

Ready... set... now preheat that oven!

**350° F**

*1.* In a mixing bowl, **mush** the butter, the half cup of confectioners' sugar and the vanilla together. Add the flour, pecans and salt. **Whirl** until all of the ingredients have **mingled** into a dough.

*2.* Roll the dough into **orbs**, that are about an inch around.

*3.* Place the **orbs** on an baking sheet covered with parchment paper.

*4.* Carefully place the baking sheet in the oven and bake away.

**15 minutes**

*5.* While you are waiting on the cookies in the oven, place the remaining confectioners' sugar in a small mixing bowl.

*6.* When the time is up, cautiously remove the baking sheet from the oven and allow the cookies to sit on the baking sheet, placed on a heat proof surface, to cool for 5 minutes. After the 5 minutes is up remove each cookie with a metal spatula and roll each cookie in the small bowl of confectioners' sugar. After they are sugared place them on a wire rack to cool off further.

## Ingredients:

1 cup butter
1/2 cup confectioners' sugar
1 teaspoon vanilla extract
2 1/4 cups all-purpose flour
1 cup pecans, chopped
1/4 teaspoon salt
1/3 cup confectioners' sugar

## What you'll need:

measuring cups
measuring spoons
mixer with beater & bowl
small mixing bowl
baking sheet
parchment paper
metal spatula
wire cooling rack

## United States of America

19

# Drop Cookies

# Anginetti Cookies

## Directions:

Ready... set... now preheat that oven!

**350° F**

**1.** In a mixing bowl, **whirl** the flour, sugar, baking powder, oil, milk, salt, lemon juice and eggs together.

**2.** Spoon the dough, by rounded teaspoons, onto a greased baking sheet, about 2 inches apart.

**3.** Carefully place the baking sheet in the oven and bake away.

**15 minutes**

**4.** When the time is up, cautiously remove the baking sheet from the oven and allow the cookies to sit on the baking sheet, placed on a heat proof surface, to cool for 5 minutes. After the 5 minutes is up remove the cookies from the baking sheet with a metal spatula and place them on a wire rack to cool off further.

**5.** For the frosting, **mush** the butter and sugar, juices and extract together in a medium mixing bowl.

**6.** Dip each cookie top into the frosting.

## Ingredients:

5 cups all-purpose flour
1 cup sugar
5 teaspoons baking powder
1 cup vegetable oil
1 cup milk
1/8 teaspoon salt
2 teaspoons lemon juice
2 eggs

**Frosting:**
3 cups confectioners' sugar
4 tablespoons butter, softened
6 tablespoons orange juice
2 teaspoons lemon juice
2 1/2 teaspoons vanilla extract

## What you'll need:

measuring cups
measuring spoons
mixer with beater & bowl

kitchen spoon
baking sheet
mediun bowl

metal spatula
wire rack

*Italy*

# Brownie Bumps

## Ingredients:

2/3 cup shortening
1 1/2 cups brown sugar, packed
1 tablespoon water
1 tablespoon vanilla extract
2 eggs
1 1/2 cups all-purpose flour
1/3 cup baking cocoa
1/2 teaspoon salt
1/4 teaspoon baking soda
2 cups semisweet chocolate chips
1/2 cup walnuts, chopped

## What you'll need:

measuring cups
measuring spoons
mixer with beater & bowl
kitchen spoon
baking sheet
metal spatula
wire cooling rack

## Directions:

Ready... set... now preheat that oven!

**375° F**

*1.* In a mixing bowl, **mush** the shortening, sugar, water, vanilla, and eggs together. Add the flour, cocoa, salt and baking soda. **Whirl** until all of the ingredients have **mingled** into a dough. Then, add in the chocolate chips and nuts, and **whirl** a few more times around.

*2.* Spoon the dough, by rounded teaspoons, onto an ungreased baking sheet, about 2 inches apart.

*3.* Carefully place the baking sheet in the oven and bake away.

**7-9 minutes**

*4.* When the time is up, cautiously remove the baking sheet from the oven and allow the cookies to sit on the baking sheet, placed on a heat proof surface, to cool for 5 minutes. After the 5 minutes is up remove the cookies from the baking sheet with a metal spatula and place them on a wire rack to cool off further.

# Butter Pecan Shortbread Cookies

## Directions:

Ready... set... now preheat that oven!

**375° F**

*1.* In a mixing bowl, **mush** the butter and sugars together. Add in the eggs, vanilla, flour, baking soda, and salt. **Whirl** until all of the ingredients have **mingled** into a dough. Then, add in the pecans, and **whirl** a few more times around.

*2.* Spoon the dough, by rounded teaspoons, onto an ungreased baking sheet, about 2 inches apart.

*3.* Carefully place the baking sheet in the oven and bake away.

**10 minutes**

*4.* When the time is up, cautiously remove the baking sheet from the oven and allow the cookies to sit on the baking sheet, placed on a heat proof surface, to cool for 5 minutes. After the 5 minutes is up remove the cookies from the baking sheet with a metal spatula and place them on a wire rack to cool off further.

## Ingredients:

1 cup butter, softened
3/4 cup sugar
3/4 cup brown sugar, packed
2 eggs
1 teaspoon vanilla extract
2 1/4 cups all-purpose flour
1 teaspoon baking soda
1/8 teaspoon salt
1 cup pecans, chopped

## What you'll need:

measuring cups
measuring spoons
mixer with beater & bowl
kitchen spoon
baking sheet
metal spatula
wire cooling rack

## United States of America

# Chocolate Chip Cookies

## Ingredients:

1 cup shortening, butter flavored
3/4 cup white sugar
3/4 cup brown sugar, packed
2 eggs
2 teaspoons mexican vanilla extract
2 1/4 cups all-purpose flour
1 teaspoon baking soda
1 teaspoon salt
2 cups milk chocolate chips

## What you'll need:

measuring cups
measuring spoons
mixer with beater & bowl
kitchen spoon
baking sheet
metal spatula
wire cooling rack

## Directions:

Ready... set... now preheat that oven!

**350° F**

**1.** In a mixing bowl, **mush** the shortening and sugars together. Add in the eggs, vanilla, flour, baking soda, and salt. **Whirl** until all of the ingredients have **mingled** into a dough. Once **mingled**, add in the chocolate chips, and **whirl** a few more times around.

**2.** Spoon the dough, by rounded teaspoons, onto a greased baking sheet, about 2 inches apart.

**3.** Carefully place the baking sheet in the oven and bake away.

**8-10 minutes**

**4.** When the time is up, cautiously remove the baking sheet from the oven and allow the cookies to sit on the baking sheet, placed on a heat proof surface, to cool for 5 minutes. After the 5 minutes is up remove the cookies from the baking sheet with a metal spatula and place them on a wire rack to cool off further.

United States of America

# Double Chocolate Chip Cookies

## Ingredients:

2 cups milk chocolate pieces, chopped
8 tablespoons butter
1 1/2 cups sugar
2 eggs
1 teaspoon vanilla extract
1 cup all-purpose flour
1/2 cup dutch-process cocoa powder
1/2 teaspoon baking soda
1/2 teaspoon salt
2 cups milk chocolate chips

## What you'll need:

measuring cups
measuring spoons
double boiler
mixer with beater & bowl
ice cream scoop
parchment paper
baking sheet
wire cooling rack

## Directions:

Ready... set... now preheat that oven!

325° F

*1.* Fill the bottom of a double boiler with some water and bring it to a boil then reduce to low heat. In the top boiler melt the chocolate and butter together and then pour the mixture into a mixing bowl.

*2.* In the mixing bowl, mix the sugar, eggs and vanilla into the melted chocolate mixture. Then slowly add in the flour, cocoa, baking soda, and salt. **Whirl** until all of the ingredients have **mingled** into a dough. Then add in the chocolate chips and **whirl** a few more times around.

*3.* Spoon the dough, with an ice cream scoop, onto a parchment lined baking sheet, about 2 inches apart.

*4.* Carefully place the baking sheet in the oven and bake away.

15 minutes

*5.* When the time is up, cautiously remove the baking sheet from the oven and allow the cookies to sit on the baking sheet, placed on a heat proof surface, to cool for 5 minutes. After the 5 minutes is up transfer the cookies, while still on the parchment paper, from the baking sheet to a wire rack to cool off further.

## United States of America

# Hickory Nut Cookies

*Hecker Nuesse Kuchen*

## Directions:

Ready... set... now preheat that oven!

**325° F**

**1.** In a mixing bowl, **mush** the eggs and sugar together. Add in the flour, baking powder, cinnamon and salt. **Whirl** until all of the ingredients have **mingled** into a dough. Then, add in the hickory nuts, and **whirl** a few more times around.

**2.** Spoon the dough, by rounded teaspoons, onto a greased baking sheet, about 2 inches apart.

**3.** Carefully place the baking sheet in the oven and bake away.

**15 minutes**

**4.** When the time is up, cautiously remove the baking sheet from the oven and allow the cookies to sit on the baking sheet, placed on a heat proof surface, to cool for 5 minutes. After the 5 minutes is up remove the cookies from the baking sheet with a metal spatula and place them on a wire rack to cool off further.

## Ingredients:

3 eggs
2 cups sugar
2/3 cup flour
1 teaspoon baking powder
1/4 teaspoon ground cinnamon
1/8 teaspoon salt
1 cup hickory nuts, chopped

## What you'll need:

measuring cups
measuring spoons
mixer with beater & bowl
kitchen spoon
baking sheet
metal spatula
wire cooling rack

*Germany*

# Lizzies

## Ingredients:

2 cups red candied cherries, halved
1/2 cup green candied cherries, halved
2 cups candied pineapple, cut in pieces
1 cup pitted dates, chopped
1 cup pound golden raisins
4 cups pecans, chopped
1/4 cup all-purpose flour
1/4 cup butter, softened
3/4 cup brown sugar, packed
2 eggs
2 cups all-purpose flour
1 1/2 teaspoons baking soda
1 tablespoon milk
1/2 cup peach brandy

## What you'll need:

measuring cups
measuring spoons
large mixing bowl
mixer with beater & bowl
kitchen spoon
baking sheet
muffin tin (optional)
metal spatula
wire cooling rack

## Directions:

Ready... set... now preheat that oven!

**275° F**

**1.** In a large mixing bowl, dust the cherries, pineapple, dates, raisins and pecans with the 1/4 cup of flour and set aside.

**2.** In a mixing bowl **mush** the butter and brown sugar together. Add in the eggs, flour, baking soda, milk and peach brandy. **Whirl** until all of the ingredients have **mingled** into a dough. Then, add the dusted cherries, pineapple, dates, raisins and pecans. **Whirl** a few more times around.

**3.** Spoon the dough, by rounded teaspoons, onto a greased baking sheet (or into a greased muffin tin).

**4.** Carefully place the baking sheet in the oven and bake away.

**18-20 minutes**

**5.** When the time is up, cautiously remove the baking sheet from the oven and allow the cookies to sit on the baking sheet, placed on a heat proof surface, to cool for 5 minutes. After the 5 minutes is up remove the cookies from the baking sheet with a metal spatula and place them on a wire rack to cool off further.

## United States of America

# Munchers

## Directions:

Ready... set... now preheat that oven!

350° F

**1.** In a mixing bowl, **mush** the butter and sugar together. Add in the eggs, vanilla, flour, baking powder, and salt. **Whirl** until all of the ingredients have **mingled** into a dough. Then, add in all of the chocolate chips, toffee bits and pecans. **Whirl** a few more times around.

**2.** Spoon the dough, by rounded teaspoons, onto a greased baking sheet, about 2 inches apart.

**3.** Carefully place the baking sheet in the oven and bake away.

10-12 minutes

**4.** When the time is up, cautiously remove the baking sheet from the oven and allow the cookies to sit on the baking sheet, placed on a heat proof surface, to cool for 5 minutes. After the 5 minutes is up remove the cookies from the baking sheet with a metal spatula and place them on a wire rack to cool off further.

## Ingredients:

1 cup butter, softened
1 1/2 cups brown sugar, packed
2 eggs
2 teaspoons vanilla extract
2 1/2 cups all-purpose flour
1 teaspoon baking powder
1/4 teaspoon salt
1 cup milk chocolate chips
1/2 cup semisweet chocolate chips
2/3 cup toffee bits
1 cup pecans, chopped

## What you'll need:

measuring cups
measuring spoons
mixer with beater & bowl
kitchen spoon
baking sheet
metal spatula
wire cooling rack

# Pecan Fudge Chewies

## Ingredients:

1/4 cup butter
1 (14 oz.) can sweetened condensed
  milk
2 cups semisweet chocolate chips
1 teaspoon vanilla extract
1 cup all-purpose flour
1/2 cup pecans, chopped
60 pecan halves

## What you'll need:

measuring cups
measuring spoons
large saucepan
mixer with beater & bowl
kitchen spoon
baking sheet
metal spatula
wire cooling rack

## Directions:

Ready... set... now preheat that oven!

**350° F**

*1.* In a large saucepan, melt the butter and chocolate chips in the milk, over medium-low heat. Stir constantly and remove from heat once melted.

*2.* Pour the chocolate and butter mixture into a mixing bowl, along with the vanilla, flour and chopped pecans. **Whirl** until all of the ingredients have **mingled** into a dough.

*3.* Spoon the dough, by rounded teaspoons, onto an ungreased baking sheet, about 2 inches apart. Then press a halved pecan into the center of each cookie.

*4.* Carefully place the baking sheet in the oven and bake away.

**7 minutes**

*5.* When the time is up, cautiously remove the baking sheet from the oven and allow the cookies to sit on the baking sheet, placed on a heat proof surface, to cool for 5 minutes. After the 5 minutes is up remove the cookies from the baking sheet with a metal spatula and place them on a wire rack to cool off further.

*United States of America*

# Pfeffernuesse

## Directions:

Ready... set... now preheat that oven!

**350° F**

**1.** In a mixing bowl, **mush** the butter and sugar together. Add in the egg, flour, baking powder, lemon peel, salt, cinnamon, nutmeg, cloves, pepper and milk. **Whirl** until all of the ingredients have **mingled** into a dough. Then, add in the walnuts and anise seed. **Whirl** a few more times around.

**2.** Spoon the dough, by rounded teaspoons, onto a greased baking sheet, about 2 inches apart.

**3.** Carefully place the baking sheet in the oven and bake away.

**15-17 minutes**

**4.** When the time is up, cautiously remove the baking sheet from the oven and allow the cookies to sit on the baking sheet, placed on a heat proof surface, to cool for 5 minutes. After the 5 minutes is up roll each cookie in the bowl of confectioners' sugar. Then place them on a wire rack to cool off further.

## Ingredients:

1/3 cup butter, softened
1/2 cup sugar
1 egg
1 2/3 cups all-purpose flour
1 1/2 teaspoon baking powder
1 teaspoon lemon peel, grated
1/2 teaspoon salt
1/4 teaspoon ground cinnamon
1 teaspoon ground nutmeg
1/8 teaspoon ground cloves
1/4 teaspoon ground white pepper
1/2 cup milk
1/2 cup walnuts, finely chopped
1 teaspoon ground anise seed
confectioners' sugar

## What you'll need:

measuring cups
measuring spoons
mixer with beater & bowl
kitchen spoon
small mixing bowl
baking sheet
metal spatula
wire cooling rack

## Germany

# Chilled Out Cookies

# Black Walnut Cookies

## Directions:

Ready... set... now preheat that oven!

**400° F**

**1.** In a small mixing bowl, dissolve the baking soda in the water, then set aside.

**2.** In another mixing bowl, **mush** the butter and sugar together. Add in the flour, baking powder/water mixture, egg, extract and walnuts. **Whirl** until all of the ingredients have **mingled** into a dough.

**3.** Divide the dough into three sections and place each section on a large piece of wax paper. Roll the dough, while in the paper, into logs and place each log in the **fridge** for an hour.

**4.** After an hour is up, remove the logs from the **fridge**. Carefully remove the wax paper and slice the logs into thin cookies. Place the cookies on a greased baking sheet.

**5.** Carefully place the baking sheet in the oven and bake away.

**9 minutes**

**6.** When the time is up, cautiously remove the baking sheet from the oven and allow the cookies to sit on the baking sheet, placed on a heat proof surface, to cool for 5 minutes. After the 5 minutes is up remove the cookies from the baking sheet and place them on a wire rack to cool off further.

## Ingredients:

1/16 teaspoon water
1/2 teaspoon baking soda
1 cup butter
1 cup dark brown sugar, packed
1 egg
1 teaspoon maple extract
2 cups all-purpose flour
1 teaspoon baking powder
1 1/2 cups black walnuts, chopped

## What you'll need:

measuring cups
measuring spoons
small mixing bowl
mixer with beater & bowl
wax paper
baking sheet
metal spatula
wire cooling rack

# Brown Sugar Walnut Cookies

## Ingredients:

1/2 cup shortening
1/2 cup butter, softened
1 cup sugar
1 cup brown sugar, packed
2 eggs
3 cups all-purpose flour
1 teaspoon baking soda
1/2 teaspoon salt
1 teaspoon ground cinnamon
1 cup walnuts, finely chopped

## What you'll need:

measuring cups
measuring spoons
mixer with beater & bowl
wax paper
baking sheet
metal spatula
wire cooling rack

## Directions:

Ready... set... now preheat that oven!

350° F

**1.** In a mixing bowl, **mush** the butter and shortening together. Add in the sugars, eggs, flour, baking soda, salt and cinnamon. **Whirl** until all of the ingredients have **mingled** into a dough. Then, add in the walnuts and **whirl** a few more times around.

**2.** On a large piece of wax paper, form and roll the dough into a log and place it in the freezer overnight.

**3.** The following day, carefully remove the log from the wax paper. Slice the log into thin cookies and place on an ungreased baking sheet, about an inch apart.

**4.** Carefully place the baking sheet in the oven and bake away.

8-10 minutes

**5.** When the time is up, cautiously remove the baking sheet from the oven and allow the cookies to sit on the baking sheet, placed on a heat proof surface, to cool for 5 minutes. After the 5 minutes is up remove the cookies from the baking sheet with a metal spatula and place them on a wire rack to cool off further.

34

United States of America

# Canadian Flag Cookies

## Directions:

**350° F**

Ready... set... now preheat that oven!

*1.* In a mixing bowl, **mush** the butter, egg white and vanilla together. Add in the flour, sugar, and baking powder. **Whirl** until all of the ingredients have **mingled** into a dough.

*2.* Divide the dough into three sections. Place two of the sections back in the mixer and add the red food coloring, mixing it until the color is spread evenly. Remove the dough from the mixer and divide into two. You should have one un-colored section and two red sections.

*3.* Place each section on a large piece of wax paper and form into individual bars, about an inch thick. Wrap up each section and place the bars in the **fridge** for an hour.

*4.* After the hour is up, remove the wax paper from the bars and stack the bars on top of each other in the following order: red, un-colored, red. Wrap the three layered bar in wax paper and place in the **fridge** for another hour.

*5.* Remove the bar from the **fridge** and slice the bar into 1/4 inch thick cookies. Place on a greased baking sheet.

*6.* Carefully place the baking sheet in the oven and bake away.

**12 minutes**

*7.* When the time is up, cautiously remove the baking sheet from the oven and allow the cookies to sit on the baking sheet, placed on a heat proof surface, to cool for 5 minutes. After the 5 minutes is up remove the cookies from the baking sheet and place them on a wire rack to cool off further.

## Ingredients:

1 cup butter, softened
1 egg white
2 teaspoons vanilla extract
2 1/2 cups all-purpose flour
1 1/2 cups sugar
1 1/2 teaspoons baking powder
1 teaspoon red food coloring

## What you'll need:

measuring cups
measuring spoons
mixer with beater & bowl
wax paper
baking sheet
metal spatula
wire cooling rack

*Canada*

# Chocolate Chunk Fudgies

## Ingredients:

2 2/3 cups semisweet chocolate, coarsely chopped
1/4 cup butter
1 3/4 cups sugar
4 eggs
1 tablespoon vanilla extract
1/2 cup cake flour
1 teaspoon baking powder
1/4 teaspoon salt
1 cup semisweet dark chocolate chips
1 cup white chocolate chips

## What you'll need:

measuring cups
measuring spoons
double boiler
mixer with beater & bowl
plastic wrap
ice cream scoop
parchment paper
baking sheet
metal spatula
wire cooling rack

## Directions:

**350° F**

Ready... set... now preheat that oven!

*1.* Fill the bottom of a double boiler with some water and bring it to a boil, then reduce the heat. In the top boiler melt the chocolate pieces and butter together, then set aside.

*2.* In a mixing bowl, mix the sugar and eggs together. Slowly add in the melted chocolate mixture, vanilla, flour, baking powder and salt. **Whirl** until all of the ingredients have **mingled** into a dough. Add in the chocolate chips. **Whirl** a few more times.

*3.* Remove the mixing bowl from the mixer and cover the top of the bowl with plastic wrap. After covered, place the bowl in the **fridge** for an hour.

*4.* After the hour is up, drop the dough, with an ice cream scoop, onto a parchment lined baking sheet, about 2 inches apart.

*5.* Carefully place the baking sheet in the oven and bake away.

**10-12 minutes**

*6.* When the time is up, cautiously remove the baking sheet from the oven and allow the cookies to sit on the baking sheet, placed on a heat proof surface, to cool for 5 minutes. After the 5 minutes is up transfer the cookies, while still on the parchment paper, from the baking sheet to a wire rack to cool off further.

## United States of America

# Chocolate Nuggets

## Directions:

Ready... set... now preheat that oven!

**375° F**

*1.* In a large saucepan melt the semisweet chocolate pieces, over low heat, stirring constantly. Remove from the heat it is fully once melted.

*2.* In a mixing bowl, **mush** the butter and sugar together. Add in the vanilla, milk, egg, salt, melted chocolate and flour. **Whirl** until all of the ingredients have **mingled** into a dough.

*3.* Remove the mixing bowl from the mixer and cover the top of the bowl with plastic wrap. After covered, place the bowl in the refridgerator for an hour.

*4.* After an hour has passed roll the dough into **orbs**, that are about an inch around.  Then roll the **orbs** in **jimmies** and place each **orb** on an ungreased baking sheet.

*5.* Carefully place the baking sheet in the oven and bake away.

**10-12 minutes**

*6.* When the time is up, cautiously remove the baking sheet from the oven and allow the cookies to sit on the baking sheet, placed on a heat proof surface, to cool for 5 minutes. After the 5 minutes is up remove the cookies from the baking sheet with a metal spatula and place them on a wire rack to cool off further.

## Ingredients:

1/3 cup semisweet chocolate chips
3/4 cup butter
1 cup sugar
1/2 teaspoon vanilla extract
2 tablespoons milk
1 egg
1/4 teaspoon salt
2 1/2 cups all-purpose flour
**jimmies**

## What you'll need:

measuring cups
measuring spoons
large saucepan
mixer with beater & bowl
plastic wrap
baking sheet
metal spatula
wire cooling rack

## United States of America

# Cowboy Cookies

## Ingredients:

1 cup butter, softened
3/4 cup sugar
3/4 cup brown sugar, packed
2 cups all-purpose flour
2 cups old-fashioned oats
1 teaspoon baking soda
1/2 teaspoon baking powder
1/2 teaspoon salt
2 eggs
1 teaspoon vanilla extract
1 1/2 cups semisweet chocolate chips
1 cup walnuts, chopped

## What you'll need:

measuring cups
measuring spoons
mixer with beater & bowl
plastic wrap
glass
baking sheet
metal spatula
wire cooling rack

## Directions:

Ready... set... now preheat that oven!

**350° F**

*1.* In a mixing bowl, **mush** the butter and sugars together. Add in the flour, oats, baking soda, baking powder, salt, eggs and vanilla. **Whirl** until all of the ingredients have **mingled** into a dough. Then, add in the chocolate chips and walnuts. **Whirl** a few more times around.

*2.* Remove the mixing bowl from the mixer and cover the top of the bowl with plastic wrap. After covered, place the bowl in the **fridge** for an hour.

*3.* After an hour has passed roll the dough into **orbs**, that are about an inch around. Place the **orbs** on a greased baking sheet and flatten each **orb** with a glass.

*4.* Carefully place the baking sheet in the oven and bake away.

**10 - 15 minutes**

*5.* When the time is up, cautiously remove the baking sheet from the oven and allow the cookies to sit on the baking sheet, placed on a heat proof surface, to cool for 5 minutes. After the 5 minutes is up remove the cookies from the baking sheet with a metal spatula and place them on a wire rack to cool off further.

*United States of America*

# Flag Cookies

## Directions:

350° F

Ready... set... now preheat that oven!

**1.** In a mixing bowl, **mush** the butter, egg white and vanilla together. Add in the flour, sugar, and baking powder. **Whirl** until all of the ingredients have **mingled** into a dough.

**2.** Divide the dough into three sections. Place one of the sections back in the mixer and add the red food coloring, mixing it until the color is spread evenly. Remove the dough from the mixer and set aside. Place another un-colored section in the mixer and add the blue food coloring, mixing it until the color is spread evenly. Remove the dough from the mixer and set aside. You should have one un-colored section, one red section and one blue section of dough.

**3.** Place each section on a large piece of wax paper and form into bars about an inch thick. Wrap each section up individually and place in the **fridge** for an hour.

**4.** Carefully remove the bars from the wax paper and stack the bars on top of each other in the following order: red, un-colored, blue. Wrap the three layered bar in wax paper and place in the **fridge** for another hour.

**5.** Remove the bar from the **fridge** and slice the bar into 1/4 inch thick cookies. Place the cookies on a greased baking sheet.

**6.** Carefully place the baking sheet in the oven and bake away.

**12 minutes**

**7.** When the time is up, cautiously remove the baking sheet from the oven and allow the cookies to sit on the baking sheet, placed on a heat proof surface, to cool for 5 minutes. After the 5 minutes is up remove the cookies from the baking sheet with a metal spatula and place them on a wire rack to cool off further.

## Ingredients:

1 cup butter, softened
1 egg white
2 teaspoons vanilla extract
2 1/2 cups all-purpose flour
1 1/2 cups sugar
1 1/2 teaspoons baking powder
1 teaspoon red food coloring
1 teaspoon blue food coloring

## What you'll need:

measuring cups
measuring spoons
mixer with beater & bowl
wax paper
baking sheet
metal spatula
wire cooling rack

## United States of America

39

# Italian Flag Cookies

## Ingredients:

2 pkgs. active dry yeast
1/4 cup warm water
2 cups butter, softened
1 cup sugar
1 egg
1/2 teaspoon almond extract
4 1/2 cups all-purpose flour
red colored sugar
green colored sugar

## What you'll need:

measuring cups
measuring spoons
small mixing bowl
mixer with beater & bowl
plastic wrap
baking sheet
metal spatula
wire cooling rack

## Directions:

Ready... set... now preheat that oven!

**375° F**

*1.* In a small mixing bowl, dissolve the yeast in the warm water.

*2.* In another mixing bowl, **mush** the butter and sugar together. Add in the egg, almond, yeast mixture, and flour. **Whirl** until all of the ingredients have **mingled** into a dough.

*3.* Remove the mixing bowl from the mixer and cover the top of the bowl with plastic wrap. After covered, place the bowl in the **fridge** for two hours.

*4.* After two hours has passed roll the dough into **orbs**, that are about an inch around. Dip one side of each **orb** in red colored sugar and the other side of each **orb** in the green colored sugar, leaving an un-sugared section in the middle. Place each **orb** on a greased baking sheet.

*5.* Carefully place the baking sheet in the oven and bake away.

**10-12 minutes**

*6.* When the time is up, cautiously remove the baking sheet from the oven and allow the cookies to sit on the baking sheet, placed on a heat proof surface, to cool for 5 minutes. After the 5 minutes is up remove the cookies from the baking sheet with a metal spatula and place them on a wire rack to cool off further.

*Italy*

# Mailanderli

## Directions:

Ready... set... now preheat that oven!

**325° F**

*1.* In a mixing bowl, **mush** the butter and sugar together. Add in the egg yolks, vanilla, lemon zest and flour. **Whirl** until all of the ingredients have **mingled** into a dough.

*2.* Remove the mixing bowl from the mixer and cover the top of the bowl with plastic wrap. After covered, place the bowl in the **fridge** for an hour.

*3.* After an hour has passed roll the dough out on a floured surface, to about 1/4 inch thick, and cut shapes out with cookie cutters.

*4.* In a small mixing bowl, beat the remaining egg. Using a pastry brush, brush the tops of each cookie with the egg.

*5.* Place the cookies on a parchment lined baking sheet. Carefully place the baking sheet in the oven and bake away.

**24 minutes**

*6.* When the time is up, cautiously remove the baking sheet from the oven and allow the cookies to sit on the baking sheet, placed on a heat proof surface, to cool for 5 minutes. After the 5 minutes is up remove the cookies from the baking sheet with a metal spatula and place them on a wire rack to cool off further.

## Ingredients:

2 cups butter, softened
1 cup sugar
6 egg yolks
1 tablespoon vanilla extract
zest of 2 lemons
5 cups all-purpose flour
1 egg

## What you'll need:

measuring cups
measuring spoons
mixer with beater & bowl
plastic wrap
rolling pin
cookie cutters
small mixing bowl
pastry brush
baking sheet
metal spatula
wire cooling rack

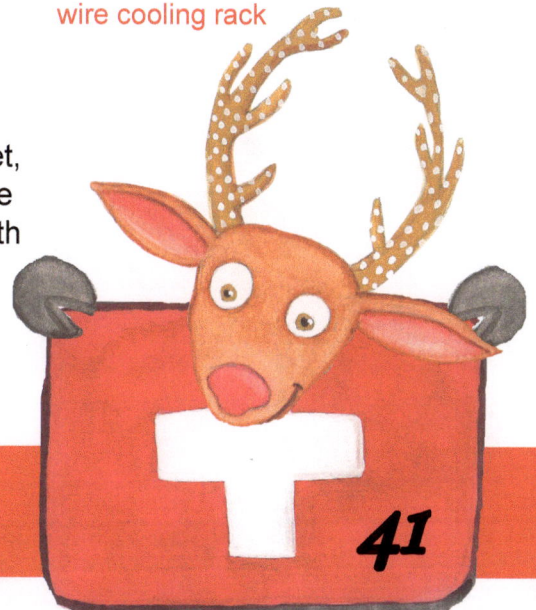

## Switzerland

41

# Mexican Flag Cookies

## Ingredients:

2 pkgs. active dry yeast
1/4 cup warm water
2 cups butter, softened
1 cup sugar
1 egg
4 1/2 cups all-purpose flour
red colored sugar
green colored sugar

## What you'll need:

measuring cups
measuring spoons
small mixing bowl
mixer with beater & bowl
plastic wrap
baking sheet
metal spatula
wire cooling rack

## Directions:

Ready... set... now preheat that oven!

**350° F**

*1.* In a small mixing bowl, dissolve the yeast in the warm water.

*2.* In another mixing bowl, **mush** the butter and sugar together. Add in the egg, yeast/water mixture, and flour. **Whirl** until all of the ingredients have **mingled** into a dough.

*3.* Remove the mixing bowl from the mixer and cover the top of the bowl with plastic wrap. After covered, place the bowl in the **fridge** for two hours.

*4.* After two hours has passed roll the dough into **orbs**, that are about an inch around. Dip one side of each **orb** in red colored sugar and the other side of each **orb** in the green colored sugar, leaving an un-sugared section in the middle. Place each **orb** on a greased baking sheet.

*5.* Carefully place the baking sheet in the oven and bake away.

**10-12 minutes**

*6.* When the time is up, cautiously remove the baking sheet from the oven and allow the cookies to sit on the baking sheet, placed on a heat proof surface, to cool for 5 minutes. After the 5 minutes is up remove the cookies from the baking sheet with a metal spatula and place them on a wire rack to cool off further.

42

*Mexico*

# Mint Chocolate Cookies

## Directions:

**375° F**

Ready... set... now preheat that oven!

**1.** In a mixing bowl, **mush** the butter, sugars, cocoa, baking powder and baking soda together. Add in the eggs, vanilla, and flour. **Whirl** until all of the ingredients have **mingled** into a dough.

**2.** Remove the mixing bowl from the mixer and cover the top of the bowl with plastic wrap. After covered, place the bowl in the **fridge** for two hours.

**3.** After two hours has passed roll the dough into **orbs**, that are about an inch around.

**4.** Place the **orbs** on an ungreased baking sheet. Carefully place the baking sheet in the oven and bake away.

**8-10 minutes**

**5.** While waiting you can start making the filling and the glaze. For the filing, in another mixing bowl, **mush** the butter and crème de menthe together. Add in the confectioners' sugar. Set aside. For the glaze, cook and stir the chocolate and cream together, in a medium saucepan, over low heat until melted. Remove the saucepan from the heat and let it stand for 20 minutes.

**6.** When the cookies are done in the oven, cautiously remove the baking sheet from the oven and allow the cookies to sit on the baking sheet, placed on a heat proof surface, to cool for 5 minutes. After the 5 minutes is up remove the cookies from the baking sheet with a metal spatula and place them on a wire rack to cool off further.

**7.** Once the cookies have cooled, spread the filling on the flat side of one cookie and then press that to the flat side of another cookie, making a sandwhich. Then, top each cookie with the glaze and place each cookie back on the wire rack, to let the glaze set completely.

## Ingredients:

1 cup butter, softened
1 cup sugar
1/2 cup brown sugar, packed
2/3 cup cocoa powder
1 1/2 teaspoon baking powder
1/4 teaspoon baking soda
3 eggs
2 teaspoon vanilla extract
2 cups all-purpose flour

**Filling:**
1/3 cup butter, softened
3 tablespoons crème de menthe
4 cups confectioners' sugar

**Glaze:**
1 cup semisweet chocolate chips
1/3 cup whipping cream

## What you'll need:

measuring cups
measuring spoons
mixer with beater & bowl
plastic wrap
medium mixing bowl
medium saucepan
baking sheet
metal spatula
wire cooling rack

## United States of America

**43**

# Norwegian Cookies

## Ingredients:

1 cup butter
1 cup sugar
1 egg
1/2 teaspoon vanilla extract
1/2 teaspoon almond extract
2 cups all-purpose flour
1/2 cup walnuts, finely chopped
red and green colored sugar

## What you'll need:

measuring cups
measuring spoons
mixer with beater & bowl
plastic wrap
glass
baking sheet
metal spatula
wire cooling rack

## Directions:

Ready... set... now preheat that oven!

**350° F**

*1.* In a mixing bowl, **mush** the butter and sugar together. Add in the egg, extracts, flour and walnuts. **Whirl** until all of the ingredients have **mingled** into a dough.

*2.* Remove the mixing bowl from the mixer and cover the top of the bowl with plastic wrap. After covered, place the bowl in the **fridge** for an hour.

*3.* After an hour has passed, roll the dough into **orbs** that are about an inch around. Place the **orbs** on a greased baking sheet and flatten each **orb** with a glass, that was dipped in the colored sugar.

*4.* Carefully place the baking sheet in the oven and bake away.

**8-10 minutes**

*5.* When the time is up, cautiously remove the baking sheet from the oven and allow the cookies to sit on the baking sheet, placed on a heat proof surface, to cool for 5 minutes. After the 5 minutes is up remove the cookies from the baking sheet with a metal spatula and place them on a wire rack to cool off further.

## Norway

# Santa's Whiskers

## Directions:

Ready... set... now preheat that oven!

**375° F**

*1.* In a mixing bowl, **mush** the butter and sugar together. Add in the flour, milk, and vanilla. **Whirl** until all of the ingredients have **mingled** into a dough. Add in the cherries and pecans, and **whirl** a few more times around.

*2.* Shape the dough into an 8 inch log, and roll the log in the coconut. After the log is coated in coconut, wrap the log in wax paper and place in the **fridge** for two hours.

*3.* After two hours have passed, carefully unwrap the log and cut the dough into 1/4 inch slices. Place the slices on an ungreased cookie sheet.

*4.* Carefully place the baking sheet in the oven and bake away.

**10-12 minutes**

*5.* When the time is up, cautiously remove the baking sheet from the oven and allow the cookies to sit on the baking sheet, placed on a heat proof surface, to cool for 5 minutes. After the 5 minutes is up remove the cookies from the baking sheet with a metal spatula and place them on a wire rack to cool off further.

## Ingredients:

3/4 cup butter
3/4 cup sugar
2 cups flour
1 tablespoon milk
1 teaspoon vanilla extract
3/4 cup candied red cherries, finely chopped
1/3 cup pecans, finely chopped
3/4 cup coconut, shredded

## What you'll need:

measuring cups
measuring spoons
mixer with beater & bowl
wax paper
baking sheet
metal spatula
wire cooling rack

## United States of America

45

# Speculaas
## *Spekulatius*

## Ingredients:

1 cup butter, softened
2 teaspoons vanilla extract
1 cup sugar
1 1/4 cups brown sugar, packed
2 eggs
3 1/2 cups all-purpose flour
2 teaspoons baking soda
2 teaspoons ground cinnamon
1 teaspoon ground nutmeg
1 teaspoon ground cloves
1/2 teaspoon ground ginger
1/2 teaspoon ground anise seed
1/8 teaspoon salt
1/2 cup almonds, sliced

## What you'll need:

measuring cups
measuring spoons
mixer with beater & bowl
wax paper
cookie cutters
speculaas mold (optional)
baking sheet
metal spatula
wire cooling rack

## Directions:

Ready... set... now preheat that oven!

**350° F**

*1.* In a mixing bowl, **mush** the butter, vanilla and sugars together. Add in the eggs, flour, baking soda, cinnamon, nutmeg, cloves, ginger, anise seed, and salt. **Whirl** until all of the ingredients have **mingled** into a dough. Then, add in the almonds, and **whirl** a few more times around.

*2.* Divide the dough into 4 equal parts, cover each with wax paper and place each part in the **fridge** overnight.

*3.* The next day, roll each section of the dough out on the counter, about 1/4 inch thick, and cut shapes out with cookie cutters. If you have a special Speculaas mold, you could use that as well. Place the cookies on a greased cookie sheet.

*4.* Carefully place the baking sheet in the oven and bake away.

**10-15 minutes**

*5.* When the time is up, cautiously remove the baking sheet from the oven and allow the cookies to sit on the baking sheet, placed on a heat proof surface, to cool for 5 minutes. After the 5 minutes is up remove the cookies from the baking sheet with a metal spatula and place them on a wire rack to cool off further.

*Holland*

# Cut Out Cookies

# Gingerbread People

## Ingredients:

1 cup butter
1 cup sugar
1 teaspoon ground cinnamon
1 teaspoon ground cloves
1 teaspoon ground nutmeg
1 teaspoon ground ginger
1/2 cup molasses
1 teaspoon vinegar
2 eggs
5 cups all-purpose flour
1 teaspoon baking soda

**Icing**:
1 cup confectioners' sugar
1/4 teaspoon vanilla extract
1 tablespoon milk

## What you'll need:

measuring cups
measuring spoons
large saucepan
mixer with beater & bowl
small mixing bowl
baking sheet
metal spatula
wire cooling rack

## Directions:

Ready... set... now preheat that oven!

**350° F**

*1.* In a large saucepan, bring the butter, sugar, cinnamon, cloves, nutmeg, ginger, and molasses to a boil, stirring constantly. Set the mixture aside.

*2.* In a mixing bowl, mix the molasses mixture with the vinegar and eggs. Add in the flour and baking soda. **Whirl** until all of the ingredients have **mingled** into a dough.

*3.* Roll the dough out on a floured surface and cut the dough with cookie cutters. Place the cut outs on an ungreased baking sheet.

*4.* Carefully place the baking sheet in the oven and bake away.

**10 minutes**

*5.* When the time is up, cautiously remove the baking sheet from the oven and allow the cookies to sit on the baking sheet, placed on a heat proof surface, to cool for 5 minutes. After the 5 minutes is up remove the cookies from the baking sheet with a metal spatula and place them on a wire rack to cool off further.

*6.* For the icing, **whirl** the sugar, vanilla and milk together in a small mixing bowl, then use the icing to decorate the gingerbread people.

## United States of America

# Piparkakut
## Ginger Cookies

## Directions:

Ready... set... now preheat that oven!

**400° F**

*1.* In a large saucepan, bring the corn syrup, cinnamon, ginger, cloves, orange rind and butter to a boil, stirring constantly. Once it reaches a boil, remove the saucepan from the heat and set it aside.

*2.* In a mixing bowl, mix the flour and baking soda. Add in the syrup/butter mixture, sugar and eggs. **Whirl** until all of the ingredients have **mingled** into a dough.

*3.* Remove the mixing bowl from the mixer and cover the top of the bowl with plastic wrap and leave it out overnight in a cool place.

*4.* The next day, roll the dough out on a floured surface and cut with cookie cutters. Place the cut outs on a greased baking sheet.

*5.* Carefully place the baking sheet in the oven and bake away.

**8 minutes**

*6.* When the time is up, cautiously remove the baking sheet from the oven and allow the cookies to sit on the baking sheet, placed on a heat proof surface, to cool for 5 minutes. After the 5 minutes is up remove the cookies from the baking sheet with a metal spatula and place them on a wire rack to cool off further.

## Ingredients:

1 cup dark corn syrup
2 teaspoons ground cinnamon
2 teaspoons ground ginger
2 teaspoons ground cloves
1 tablespoon grated orange rind
1 1/4 cups butter
7 cups all-purpose flour
3 teaspoons baking soda
1/4 cups sugar
3 eggs

## What you'll need:

measuring cups
measuring spoons
large saucepan
mixer with beater & bowl
plastic wrap
baking sheet
metal spatula
wire cooling rack

## Finland

49

# Off the Press Cookies

# Cream Cheese Cookies

## Directions:

Ready... set... now preheat that oven!

**325° F**

*1.* In a mixing bowl, **mush** the shortening and cream cheese together. Add in the sugar, egg yolk, vanilla, flour, salt and cinnamon. **Whirl** until all of the ingredients have **mingled** into a dough.

*2.* Press the dough into a cookie press and press the cookies directly on to an ungreased cookies sheet. Then sprinkle each cookie with the colored sugars.

*3.* Carefully place the baking sheet in the oven and bake away.

**10-12 minutes**

*4.* When the time is up, cautiously remove the baking sheet from the oven and allow the cookies to sit on the baking sheet, placed on a heat proof surface, to cool for 5 minutes. After the 5 minutes is up remove the cookies from the baking sheet with a metal spatula and place them on a wire rack to cool off further.

## Ingredients:

1 cup shortening
1 (3 oz.) package cream cheese, softened
1 cup sugar
1 egg yolk
1 teaspoon vanilla extract
2 1/2 cups all-purpose flour
1/2 teaspoon salt
1/4 teaspoon ground cinnamon
red and green colored sugar

## What you'll need:

measuring cups
measuring spoons
mixer with beater & bowl
cookie press
baking sheet
metal spatula
wire cooling rack

## United States of America

# Spritz

## Ingredients:

1 cup butter, softened
2/3 cup sugar
3 egg yolks
1 teaspoon vanilla extract
2 1/2 cups all-purpose flour
red and green colored sugar

## What you'll need:

measuring cups
measuring spoons
mixer with beater & bowl
cookie press
baking sheet
metal spatula
wire cooling rack

## Directions:

Ready... set... now preheat that oven!

**400° F**

*1.* In a mixing bowl, **mush** the butter, sugar, egg yolks and vanilla together. Add in the flour. **Whirl** until all of the ingredients have **mingled** into a dough.

*2.* Press the dough into a cookie press and press the cookies directly on to an ungreased cookies sheet. Then sprinkle each cookie with the colored sugars.

*3.* Carefully place the baking sheet in the oven and bake away.

**7-10 minutes**

*4.* When the time is up, cautiously remove the baking sheet from the oven and allow the cookies to sit on the baking sheet, placed on a heat proof surface, to cool for 5 minutes. After the 5 minutes is up remove the cookies from the baking sheet with a metal spatula and place them on a wire rack to cool off further.

## Germany

# Frosted Cookies

# Anisettes

## Ingredients:

1 cup butter, softened
3/4 cups sugar
1 teaspoon anise extract
1 teaspoon lemon extract
3 cups all-purpose flour
3 teaspoons baking powder
1/4 teaspoon salt
2 eggs

**For the glaze:**
4 tablespoons milk
2 cups confectioners' sugar
**jimmies**

## What you'll need:

measuring cups
measuring spoons
mixer with beater & bowl
baking sheet
metal spatula
wire cooling rack
small saucepan
kitchen spoon

## Directions:

Ready... set... now preheat that oven!

*1.* In a mixing bowl, **mush** the butter and sugar together. Add in the extracts, flour, baking powder, salt and eggs. **Whirl** until all of the ingredients have **mingled** into a dough.

*2.* Roll the dough into **orbs**, that are about an inch around and place the **orbs** on an ungreased baking sheet, about 2 inches apart.

*3.* Carefully place the baking sheet in the oven and bake away.

*4.* When the time is up, cautiously remove the baking sheet from the oven and allow the cookies to sit on the baking sheet, placed on a heat proof surface, to cool for 5 minutes. After the 5 minutes is up remove the cookies from the baking sheet with a metal spatula and place them on a wire rack to cool off further.

*5.* In a small saucepan, for the glaze, slowly stir the milk into the confectioners' sugar, and cook over low heat (you may need to add more milk, until you have a thin enough glaze).

*6.* Spread the glaze over the cookies with a kitchen spoon and immediately top each cookie with **jimmies**.

*Italy*

# Bon Bons

## Directions:

375° F

Ready... set... now preheat that oven!

**1.** In a mixing bowl, **mush** the butter, sugar, milk and vanilla together. Add in the flour and salt. **Whirl** until all of the ingredients have **mingled** into a dough.

**2.** Choose a filling option (chocolate chunk, almond paste (cut into 1/4 inch slices), dried fruit or a whole almond) and shape the dough around the filling to form **orbs**, that are about an inch around. Place the **orbs** on an ungreased baking sheet, about 1 inch apart.

**3.** Carefully place the baking sheet in the oven and bake away.

10-12 minutes

**4.** When the time is up, cautiously remove the baking sheet from the oven and allow the cookies to sit on the baking sheet, placed on a heat proof surface, to cool for 5 minutes. After the 5 minutes is up remove the cookies from the baking sheet with a metal spatula and place them on a wire rack to cool off further.

**5.** In a small mixing bowl stir all of the vanilla frosting ingredients together. Mix until smooth.

**6.** In another small mixing bowl stir all of the chocolate frosting ingredients together. Mix until smooth.

**7.** Dip the top of each cookie into the frosting of your choice and then immediately top with a topping of your choice.

## Ingredients:

1 cup butter, softened
2/3 cup confectioners' sugar
1/4 cup milk
1 teaspoon vanilla extract
3 cups all-purpose flour
1/8 teaspoon salt

**For the filling:**
chocolate chunks, almond paste, dired fruit, or whole almonds

**For the vanilla frosing:**
1 cup confectioners' sugar
1 1/2 tablespoons milk
1 teaspoon vanilla

**For the chocolate frosing:**
1 oz. unsweetened baking chocolate, melted and cooled
1 cup confectioners' sugar
2 tablespoons milk
1 teaspoon vanilla extract

**For the toppings:**
chopped nuts, coconut, colored sugar, or **jimmies**

## What you'll need:

measuring cups, measuring spoons, mixer with beater & bowl, baking sheet, metal spatula, wire cooling rack, two small mixing bowls

## United States of America

55

# Buried Cherry Cookies

## Ingredients:

1/2 cup butter
1 cup sugar
1/4 teaspoon baking powder
1/4 teaspoon baking soda
1/4 teaspoon salt
1 egg
1 1/2 teaspoons vanilla extract
1/2 cup cocoa powder
1 1/2 cups all-purpose flour
1 (10 oz.) jar maraschino cherries
   (reserve the juice)

**For the glaze:**
1 cup semisweet chocolate chips
1/2 cup sweetened condensed milk
4 teaspoons reserved cherry juice

## What you'll need:

measuring cups
measuring spoons
mixer with beater & bowl
baking sheet
metal spatula
wire cooling rack
small saucepan
kitchen spoon

## Directions:

Ready... set... now preheat that oven!

**350° F**

*1.* In a mixing bowl, **mush** the butter and sugar together. Add in the baking powder, baking soda, salt, egg, vanilla, cocoa, and flour. **Whirl** until all of the ingredients have **mingled** into a dough.

*2.* Roll the dough into **orbs**, that are about an inch around and place the **orbs** on an ungreased baking sheet, about 2 inches apart. Then, using your thumb, make an indent in the center of each **orb** and press a cherry piece in the middle of each indent.

*3.* Carefully place the baking sheet in the oven and bake away.

**10 minutes**

*4.* When the time is up, cautiously remove the baking sheet from the oven and allow the cookies to sit on the baking sheet, placed on a heat proof surface, to cool for 5 minutes. After the 5 minutes is up remove the cookies from the baking sheet with a metal spatula and place them on a wire rack to cool off further.

*5.* In a small saucepan, for the glaze, slowly stir the chocolate and milk, while cooking over low heat. When it's fully melted stir in the cherry juice.

*6.* To glaze the cookies, spoon 1 teaspoon of the glaze over each cookie.

## United States of America

# Chocolate Sugar Cookies

## Directions:

**350° F**

Ready... set... now preheat that oven!

**1.** In a mixing bowl, **mush** the butter, sugar, eggs and vanilla together. Add in the flour, cocoa, baking powder and salt. **Whirl** until all of the ingredients have **mingled** into a dough.

**2.** Divide the dough in half and wrap each half in plastic wrap. Place the wrapped dough in the **fridge** for an hour.

**3.** After the hour is up, remove one dough half from the **fridge** and roll the dough on a floured surface to about an 1/4 inch thick. Cut the dough with cookie cutters and place the cookies on a baking sheet lined with parchment paper.

**4.** Repeat this process with the remaining dough.

**5.** Carefully place the baking sheet in the oven and bake away.

**10-12 minutes**

**6.** When the time is up, cautiously remove the baking sheet from the oven and allow the cookies to sit on the baking sheet, placed on a heat proof surface, to cool for 5 minutes. After the 5 minutes is up remove the cookies from the baking sheet with a metal spatula and place them on a wire rack to cool off further.

**7.** After the cookies have cooled completely, for the icing, beat the egg whites and lemon juice in a large mixing bowl. Add the confectioners' sugar and food coloring (if desired).

**8.** Spread the icing on the cookies with a rubber spatula. Use the icing immediately, as it will harden when it is exposed to the air.

## Ingredients:

1 cup butter, softened
1 3/4 cups sugar
2 eggs
2 teaspoons vanilla extract
2 3/4 cups all-purpose flour
3/4 cup dutch-processed cocoa powder
1 teaspoon baking powder
1/2 teaspoon salt

**For the icing:**
2 egg whites
2 teaspoons lemon juice
3 cups confectioners' sugar
food coloring (optional)

## What you'll need:

measuring cups
measuring spoons
mixer with beater & bowl
plastic wrap
parchment paper
large mixing bowl
baking sheet
metal spatula
wire cooling rack
rubber spatula

## United States of America

# Lemon Sugar Cookies

## Ingredients:

1 cup butter, softened
2 cups sugar
2 eggs
1 teaspoon grated lemon peel
2 tablespoons lemon juice
1 tablespoon milk
1 teaspoon vanilla extract
5 cups all-purpose flour
4 teaspoons baking powder
1/2 teaspoon salt

**For the frosting:**
3 cups confectioners' sugar
1 teaspoon vanilla extract
1/4 cup water
2 drops of yellow food coloring

## What you'll need:

measuring cups
measuring spoons
mixer with beater & bowl
plastic wrap
baking sheet
metal spatula
wire cooling rack
large mixing bowl
rubber spatula

## Directions:

Ready... set... now preheat that oven!

**350° F**

*1.* In a mixing bowl, **mush** the butter and sugar together. Add in the eggs, lemon peel, lemon juice, milk, vanilla, flour, baking powder, and salt. **Whirl** until all of the ingredients have **mingled** into a dough.

*2.* Remove the mixing bowl from the mixer and cover the top of the bowl with plastic wrap. After covered, place the bowl in the **fridge** for 2 hours.

*3.* After two hours have passed roll the dough out on a floured surface, to about 3/8 inch thick, and cut shapes out with cookie cutters. Place the cut outs on a parchment lined baking sheet.

*4.* Carefully place the baking sheet in the oven and bake away.

**10-14 minutes**

*5.* When the time is up, cautiously remove the baking sheet from the oven and allow the cookies to sit on the baking sheet, placed on a heat proof surface, to cool for 5 minutes. After the 5 minutes is up remove the cookies from the baking sheet with a metal spatula and place them on a wire rack to cool off further.

*6.* In a large mixing bowl, for the frosting, mix the confectioners' sugar, vanilla, water and food coloring, until smooth. Then, using a rubber spatula, spread the frosting on the top of each cookie.

## United States of America

# Sugar Cookies

## Directions:

Ready... set... now preheat that oven!

**375° F**

*1.* In a mixing bowl, **mush** the butter, sugar, egg, milk and vanilla together. Add in the flour, baking powder, and salt. **Whirl** until all of the ingredients have **mingled** into a dough.

*2.* Remove the mixing bowl from the mixer and cover the top of the bowl with plastic wrap. After covered, place the bowl in the **fridge** for 1 hour.

*3.* After an hour has passed roll the dough out on a floured surface, to about 1/4 inch thick, and cut shapes out with cookie cutters. Place the cut outs on an ungreased baking sheet.

*4.* Carefully place the baking sheet in the oven and bake away.

**8-9 minutes**

*5.* When the time is up, cautiously remove the baking sheet from the oven and allow the cookies to sit on the baking sheet, placed on a heat proof surface, to cool for 5 minutes. After the 5 minutes is up remove the cookies from the baking sheet with a metal spatula and place them on a wire rack to cool off further.

*6.* For the frosting, in a large mixing bowl, **mush** the cream cheese, butter, vanilla, food coloring and sugar together.

*7.* Then, using a rubber spatula, spread the frosting on top of each cookie.

## Ingredients:

2/3 cup butter, softened
3/4 cup sugar
1 egg
1 tablespoon milk
1 teaspoon vanilla extract
2 cups all-purpose flour
1 teaspoon baking powder
1/4 teaspoon salt

**For the frosting:**
2 (3 oz.) pkgs. cream cheese, softened
1/2 cup butter, softened
2 teaspoons vanilla extract
4 1/2 cups confectioners' sugar
food coloring (optional)

## What you'll need:

measuring cups
measuring spoons
mixer with beater & bowl
plastic wrap
baking sheet
metal spatula
wire cooling rack
large mixing bowl
rubber spatula

## United States of America

59

# Handiwork Required Cookies

# Alfajores

## Directions:

Ready... set... now preheat that oven!

*1.* In a mixing bowl, **mush** the butter and sugars. Add in the salt, extracts, almonds and flour. **Whirl** until all of the ingredients have **mingled** into a dough.

*2.* Remove the mixing bowl from the mixer and cover the top of the bowl with plastic wrap. After covered, place the bowl in the **fridge** for 30 minutes.

*3.* For the filling, heat the brown sugar and cream in a medium saucepan, stirring with a wooden spoon. As the mixture is cooking, use a pastry brush (that has been dipped in water) to wipe away the sugar crystals that form on the inside of the pan. Place the candy thermometer in the mixture and continue to heat it until it reaches the soft ball stage (238-240 degrees F). Remove the mixture from the heat and cool it down to 110 degrees F. Then stir in the butter and beat until the mixture has thickened. Add the vanilla and set aside.

*4.* Remove the dough from the **fridge** and roll the dough out on a floured surface. Cut 1/4 inch thick circles with cookie cutters. Place the cut outs on an a parchment lined baking sheet.

*5.* Carefully place the baking sheet in the oven and bake away.

12-14 minutes

*6.* When the time is up, cautiously remove the baking sheet from the oven and allow the cookies to sit on the baking sheet, placed on a heat proof surface, to cool for 5 minutes. After the 5 minutes is up remove the cookies from the baking sheet with a metal spatula and place them on a wire rack to cool off further.

*7.* To assemble, spread the filling on the flat side of a cookie and top with another cookie, flat side down. Dust the cookies with confectioners' sugar.

## Ingredients:

1 1/2 cups butter
1 cup confectioners' sugar
2 tablespoons sugar
1/4 teaspoon salt
1/2 teaspoon vanilla extract
1/4 teaspoon almond extract
1/3 cup almonds, ground
3 cups all-purpose flour

### For the filling:

2 cups brown sugar, packed
1 cup light cream
3 tablespoons butter
1/2 teaspoon vanilla extract
extra confectioners' sugar

## What you'll need:

measuring cups
measuring spoons
mixer with beater & bowl
medium saucepan
wooden spoon
candy thermometer
pastry brush
plastic wrap
cookie cutters
parchment paper
baking sheet
metal spatula
wire cooling rack
kitchen spoon

*Peru*

# Candy Canes

## Ingredients:

1 cup butter
1 cup confectioners' sugar
1 egg
1 teaspoon vanilla extract
3/4 teaspoon peppermint
  extract
2 1/2 cups all-purpose flour
1 teaspoon salt
1/2 teaspoon red food coloring

**For the topping:**
1/2 cup crushed peppermint
  candy
1/2 cup sugar

## What you'll need:

measuring cups
measuring spoons
mixer with beater & bowl
plastic wrap
baking sheet
small mixing bowl
metal spatula
wire cooling rack

## Directions:

375° F

Ready... set... now preheat that oven!

*1.* In a mixing bowl, **mush** the butter, sugar, egg and extracts together. Add in the flour and salt. **Whirl** until all of the ingredients have **mingled** into a dough. Divide the dough in half, and return half of the dough to the mixer and add the red food coloring.

*2.* Shape each dough section into a ball and wrap each in plastic wrap. Place the wrapped dough balls in the **fridge** for two hours.

*3.* After the two hours is up remove both dough balls from the **fridge** and roll the first dough out on a floured surface. Cut the dough into 4 inch strips. Repeat the process again for the remaining dough. So, you will have red and plain dough strips.

*4.* Take a red strip and a plain strip and place them side by side. Twist them together like a rope and press the ends together gently. Place each twisted rope on a greased baking sheet and curve the top of each rope to form a cane. Continue with this process until all of the dough strips have been twisted together.

*5.* Carefully place the baking sheet in the oven and bake away.

*6.* In a small bowl, mix the peppermint candy and sugar together. Set aside.

9 minutes

*7.* When the time is up, cautiously remove the baking sheet from the oven and allow the cookies to sit on the baking sheet, placed on a heat proof surface, to cool for 1 minute. After the minute is up remove the cookies from the baking sheet and place them on a wire rack to cool off further. Then sprinkle each cookie with the candy and sugar topping.

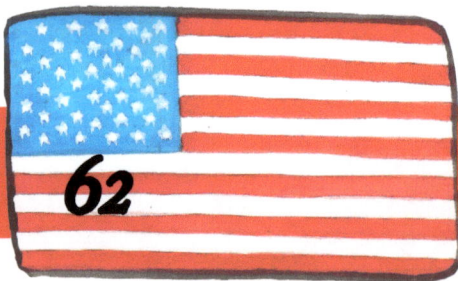

*United States of America*

# Chocolate Mint Sandwiches

## Directions:

**325° F**

Ready... set... now preheat that oven!

*1.* In a mixing bowl, **mush** the butter, sugar and vanilla together. Add in the flour, cocoa and salt. **Whirl** until all of the ingredients have **mingled** into a dough. Divide the dough in half, and place each half on a large piece (about 16 inches long) of parchment paper.

*2.* Shape each dough section into a log, about 10- 2 inches long and 2 inches wide. Wrap each log up tight and place the logs in the **fridge** to chill for 2 hours.

*3.* After the two hours is up remove both logs from the **fridge** and slice the logs into 1/2 inch thick cookies. Place each cookie on a parchment paper lined baking sheet.

*4.* Carefully place the baking sheet in the oven and bake away.

**15-20 minutes**

*5.* When the time is up, cautiously remove the baking sheet from the oven and allow the cookies to sit on the baking sheet, placed on a heat proof surface, to cool for 5 minutes. After the 5 minutes is up remove the cookies from the baking sheet with a metal spatula and place them on a wire rack to cool off further.

*6.* For the filling, fill the bottom of a double boiler with some water and in the top boiler melt the chocolate and cream, stirring constantly with a rubber spatula. When the mixture is melted add the peppermint, and take it off the heat. Set it aside to thicken, for about 30 minutes.

*7.* Once the filling has thickened, take one cookie (flat side up) and spread a tablespoon of filling on it. Then take another cookie and place it flat side down on top of the filling. Repeat until all of the cookies have been filled.

## Ingredients:

1 cup butter, softened
1 cup sugar
1 teaspoon vanilla extract
2 cups all-purpose flour
1/2 cup cocoa powder
1/4 teaspoon salt

**For the filling:**
1 cup semisweet chocolate chips
1/2 cup heavy cream
1/2 teaspoon peppermint extract

## What you'll need:

measuring cups
measuring spoons
mixer with beater & bowl
parchment paper
baking sheet
metal spatula
wire cooling rack
double boiler
rubber spatula
kitchen spoon

## United States of America

# Chocolate Whoopie Pies

## Ingredients:

3/4 cup butter, softened
3/4 cup sugar
1 egg
1 teaspoon vanilla extract
1/4 cup buttermilk
1/2 cup lukewarm water
1 3/4 cups all-purpose flour
3/4 cup dutch-processed
    cocoa powder
1 teaspoon baking powder
1/4 teaspoon baking soda
1/4 teaspoon salt

**For the filling**:
1/4 cup vegetable shortening
1/4 cup butter, softened
1 cup confectioners' sugar
1 1/2 teaspoons vanilla extract
1/2 cup light corn syrup

## What you'll need:

measuring cups
measuring spoons
mixer with beater & bowl
large mixing bowl
ice cream scoop
parchment paper
baking sheet
metal spatula
wire cooling rack
kitchen spoon

## Directions:

Ready... set... now preheat that oven!

**375° F**

*1.* In a mixing bowl, **mush** the butter and sugar together. Add in the egg, vanilla, buttermilk, water, flour, cocoa, baking powder, baking soda, and salt. **Whirl** until all of the ingredients have **mingled** into a dough.

*2.* Drop the dough, with an ice cream scoop, onto a parchment lined baking sheet, about 2 inches apart. Then, with the back of a kitchen spoon, smooth the top of each cookie.

*3.* Carefully place the baking sheet in the oven and bake away.

**9-10 minutes**

*4.* When the time is up, cautiously remove the baking sheet from the oven and allow the cookies to sit on the baking sheet, placed on a heat proof surface, to cool for 5 minutes. After the 5 minutes is up remove the cookies from the baking sheet with a metal spatula and place them on a wire rack to cool off further.

*5.* For the filling, in a mixing bowl, **mush** the shortening and butter together. Slowly add in the confectioners' sugar. Then, add in the vanilla and corn syrup.

*6.* Once the cookies have cooled, take one cookie and spread a heaping tablespoon of filling on the flat side of the cookie. Then, top that filling with the flat side of another cookie.

## United States of America

# Florentines

## Directions:

Ready... set... now preheat that oven!

**1.** In a medium saucepan, bring the butter, milk, sugar, and honey to rolling boil, stirring occasionally. Remove from heat.

**2.** In a mixing bowl, mix the almonds, fruits and peels. Add the honey mixture and 1/4 cup of flour. **Whirl** until all of the ingredients have **mingled** into a dough. You may add more flour if the mixture is on the liquid side, until it becomes more dough like.

**3.** Spoon the dough, by rounded tablespoons, onto a greased and floured baking sheet, about 3 inches apart. With the back of a kitchen spoon, spread the dough out into 3 inch circles.

**4.** Carefully place the baking sheet in the oven and bake away.

8-10 minutes

**5.** When the time is up, cautiously remove the baking sheet from the oven and allow the cookies to sit on the baking sheet, placed on a heat proof surface, to cool for 1 minute. After the minute is up remove the cookies from the baking sheet with a metal spatula and transfer them on to wax paper to cool off further.

**6.** In a small saucepan, for the icing, melt the chocolate and shortening together, over low heat. Set aside.

**7.** Once the cookies are completely cooled, spread 1 teaspoon of the icing, on the top of each cookie. Then, when the icing is almost set, use the tines of a kitchen fork to draw wavy lines in the icing, for decoration.

## Ingredients:

1/3 cup butter
1/3 cup milk
1/4 cup sugar
2 tablespoons honey
1 cup almonds, finely chopped
1/2 cup mixed candied fruits & peels, finely chopped
1/2 cup all-purpose flour

**For the icing:**
3/4 cup semisweet chocolate chips
2 tablespoons shortening

## What you'll need:

measuring cups
measuring spoons
medium saucepan
mixer with beater & bowl
baking sheet
metal spatula
wax paper
small saucepan
kitchen spoon
kitchen fork

NOTE: These cookies should be stored in the fridge.

*Italy*

# Half Moons

## Ingredients:

1 cup butter, softened
1 3/4 cups sugar
4 eggs
1/2 teaspoon vanilla extract
1/4 teaspoon lemon extract
1/2 cup milk
2 1/2 cups all-purpose flour
2 1/2 cups cake flour
1 teaspoon baking powder
1/2 teaspoon salt

**For the glaze:**
4 cups confectioners' sugar
1/2 cup hot water
2 tablespoons light corn syrup
1/2 teaspoon vanilla extract
1/3 cup semisweet chocolate
   chips

## What you'll need:

measuring cups
measuring spoons
mixer with beater & bowl
ice cream scoop
kitchen spoon
parchment paper
baking sheet
metal spatula
wire cooling rack
heatproof bowl
small saucepan

## Directions:

375° F

Ready... set... now preheat that oven!

**1.** In a mixing bowl, **mush** the butter and sugar together. Add in the eggs, extracts, milk, flours, baking powder and salt. **Whirl** until all of the ingredients have **mingled** into a dough.

**2.** Drop the dough, with an ice cream scoop, on to a parchment lined baking sheet, about 3 inches apart. Then, with the back of a kitchen spoon, spread the batter into a 2 1/2 inch round cookie.

**3.** Carefully place the baking sheet in the oven and bake away.

15-18 minutes

**4.** When the time is up, cautiously remove the baking sheet from the oven and allow the cookies to sit on the baking sheet, placed on a heat proof surface, to cool for 5 minutes. After the 5 minutes is up remove the cookies from the baking sheet with a metal spatula and place them on a wire rack to cool off further.

**5.** For the glaze, in a mixing bowl, **whirl** the confectioners' sugar, water, syrup, and vanilla together (you may need to add more sugar or more water depending on the consistency of the frosting as you'll want a spreadable consistency).

**6.** Remove 1/2 cup of the frosting and place it in a heatproof bowl, along with the chopped chocolate. Place the bowl over a saucepan of simmering water until the chocolate melts. Remove the saucepan from the heat and set aside.

**7.** To apply the glaze, turn each cookie over so that the bottoms are up. Ice half of each cookie with the white frosting, and then go back and ice the remaining half of each cookie with the chocolate frosting.

## United States of America

# Honey Walnut Balls

## Directions:

350° F

Ready... set... now preheat that oven!

*1.* In a medium saucepan, combine the honey, 1/4 cup of sugar, 1/4 cup of orange juice, and cinnamon sitck. Bring to a boil, then reduce the heat and boil gently for 5 minutes. Remove the saucepan from the heat and set it aside. Discard the cinnamon stick.

*2.* For the nut filling, in a medium mixing bowl, mix together the walnuts, orange peel and 1/4 cup of the honey/sugar syrup mixture (retain the rest of syrup for later).

*3.* In another mixing bowl, **mush** the butter and 1/2 cup of sugar together. Add in the flour, 1/4 cup of orange juice, brandy, baking powder, baking soda, cinnamon, cloves and nutmeg. **Whirl** until all of the ingredients have **mingled** into a dough. Set aside.

*4.* Roll the dough into **orbs**, that are about 1 1/4 inches around. Place each orb on a greased baking sheet and press a hole in the center of each ball. In the hole, place 1/2 teaspoon of the nut filling, and then bring the dough up and over the filling to completely enclose it. Place the seam side down. With a kitchen knife, make an X, only lightly scoring the surface of each cookie.

*5.* Carefully place the baking sheet in the oven and bake away.

18-20 minutes

*6.* When the time is up, cautiously remove the baking sheet from the oven and allow the cookies to sit on the baking sheet, placed on a heat proof surface, to cool for 1 minute. After the minute is up brush the top of each cookie with some of the reserved warm syrup mixture and then sprinkle the cookies with the walnuts. Afterward, place them on a wire rack to cool off further.

## Ingredients:

1/3 cup honey
3/4 cup sugar, divided
   (1/4 cup, 1/2 cup)
1/2 cup orange juice, divided
   (1/4 cup, 1/4 cup)
1 2" cinnamon stick
1 cup ground walnuts
1/2 teaspoon orange peel,
   finely shredded
1 cup butter
3 cups all-purpose flour
2 tablespoons brandy
3/4 teaspoon baking powder
1/4 teaspoon baking soda
1/2 teaspoon ground cinnamon
1/4 teaspoon ground cloves
1/4 teaspoon ground nutmeg
1/2 cup walnuts, finely chopped

## What you'll need:

measuring cups
measuring spoons
small saucepan
medium mixing bowl
mixer with beater & bowl
kitchen knife
baking sheet
metal spatula
pastry brush

*Greece*

# Kourabiedes
## Almond Crescents

## Ingredients:

1 cup butter, softened
2 tablespoons confectioners' sugar
1 egg yolk
1 tablespoon brandy
1/2 cup almonds, ground
2 cups all-purpose flour
1/2 teaspoon baking powder
whole cloves
2 cups confectioners' sugar

## What you'll need:

measuring cups
measuring spoons
mixer with beater & bowl
baking sheet
metal spatula
wire cooling rack

## Directions:

Ready... set... now preheat that oven!

**325° F**

*1.* In a mixing bowl, **mush** the butter and sugar together. Add in the egg yolk, brandy, almonds, flour and baking powder. **Whirl** until all of the ingredients have **mingled** into a dough.

*2.* Shape the dough into **orbs**, that are about an inch around, and roll each **orb** into a 3 inch rope. Place each rope on an ungreased baking sheet, about 2 inches apart, and shape each rope into a crescent.

*3.* Place a whole clove in each crescent.

*4.* Carefully place the baking sheet in the oven and bake away.

**6-8 minutes**

*5.* When the time is up, cautiously remove the baking sheet from the oven and allow the cookies to sit on the baking sheet, placed on a heat proof surface, to cool for 5 minutes. After the 5 minutes is up remove the cookies from the baking sheet with a metal spatula and place them on a wire rack.

*6.* Dust each crescent with confectioners' sugar and allow the cookies to cool off further.

# Love Knots

## Directions:

Ready... set... now preheat that oven!

350° F

*1.* In a mixing bowl, **mush** the butter and sugar together. Add in the eggs, lemon, flour and baking powder. **Whirl** until all of the ingredients have **mingled** into a dough.

*2.* Shape the dough into thin ropes, about 5 inches long and then tie the ropes into a knot.

*3.* Place the knots on a greased baking sheet.

*4.* Carefully place the baking sheet in the oven and bake away.

8-10 minutes

*5.* When the time is up, cautiously remove the baking sheet from the oven and allow the cookies to sit on the baking sheet, placed on a heat proof surface, to cool for 5 minutes. After the 5 minutes is up remove the cookies from the baking sheet with a metal spatula and place them on a wire rack.

*6.* Dust each knot with confectioners' sugar and allow the cookies to cool off further.

## Ingredients:

1/2 cup butter, softened
1/2 cup sugar
3 eggs
2 teaspoons lemon extract
3 cups all-purpose flour
3 teaspoons baking powder
confectioners' sugar

## What you'll need:

measuring cups
measuring spoons
mixer with beater & bowl
baking sheet
metal spatula
wire cooling rack

*Italy*

# Meringue Cookies

## Ingredients:

3 large egg whites
1/4 teaspoon cream of tartar
3/4 cup sugar, superfine
1/4 teaspoon vanilla extract

## What you'll need:

measuring cups
measuring spoons
mixer with beater & bowl
kitchen spoon
pastry bag & 1/2 inch tip
parchment paper
baking sheet
metal spatula
wire cooling rack

## Directions:

Ready... set... now preheat that oven!

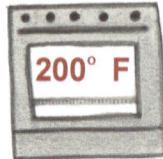

**200° F**

**1.** In a mixing bowl, **whirl** the egg whites on the low-medium mixer setting. Add in the cream of tartar and **whirl** until the egg whites start to form soft peaks. After peaks start to form, slowly add the sugar, a very little at a time, and beat on medium-high speed until the meringue can hold very stiff peaks. At this point you can add in the vanilla and **whirl** a little more.

**2.** Spoon the meringue into a pastry bag with a 1/2 inch tip. Pipe 2 1/2 inch rounds of meringues onto a baking sheet lined with parchment paper.
**Tip:** place a little meringue between the parchment paper and baking sheet to prevent the paper from sliding

**4.** Carefully place the baking sheet in the oven and bake away.

**90-105 minutes**

**5.** When the time is up, turn off the oven, open the oven door and leave the meringues to dry overnight.

**6.** The following morning, you can remove the meringues from the oven.

70

## United States of America

# Peanut Butter Cookies

## Directions:

Ready... set... now preheat that oven!

**375° F**

**1.** In a mixing bowl, **mush** the butters, sugars, eggs and vanilla together. Add in the flour, baking soda and salt. **Whirl** until all of the ingredients have **mingled** into a dough.

**2.** Remove the mixing bowl from the mixer and cover the top of the bowl with plastic wrap. After covered, place the bowl in the **fridge** for 1 hour.

**3.** After an hour has passed shape the dough into **orbs**, that are about an inch around, and roll each **orb** in sugar. Then, place the **orbs** on an ungreased baking sheet, about 2 inches apart.

**3.** Flatten each **orb** by making crisscross marks with the tines of a kitchen fork.

**4.** Carefully place the baking sheet in the oven and bake away.

**8 minutes**

**5.** When the time is up, cautiously remove the baking sheet from the oven and allow the cookies to sit on the baking sheet, placed on a heat proof surface, to cool for 5 minutes. After the 5 minutes is up remove the cookies from the baking sheet with a metal spatula and place them on a wire rack to cool off further.

## Ingredients:

1 cup peanut butter
1 cup butter, softened
1 cup sugar
1 cup brown sugar, packed
2 eggs
1 teaspoon vanilla extract
2 1/2 cups all-purpose flour
1 teaspoon baking soda
1/2 teaspoon salt
extra sugar

## What you'll need:

measuring cups
measuring spoons
mixer with beater & bowl
kithen fork
baking sheet
metal spatula
wire cooling rack

## United States of America

# Peppermint Whoopie Pies

## Ingredients:

3/4 cup butter, softened
3/4 cup sugar
1 egg
1 teaspoon vanilla extract
1/4 cup buttermilk
1/2 cup lukewarm water
1 3/4 cups all-purpose flour
3/4 cup dutch-processed cocoa powder
1 teaspoon baking powder
1/4 teaspoon baking soda
1/4 teaspoon salt

**For the filling:**
1 cup butter, softened
1 teaspoon vanilla extract
1 (7oz.) jar of marshmallow fluff
2 cups confectioners' sugar
6 drops of red food coloring
1/3 cup crushed candy canes

## What you'll need:

measuring cups
measuring spoons
mixer with beater & bowl
large mixing bowl
ice cream scoop
parchment paper
baking sheet
metal spatula
wire cooling rack
kitchen spoon

## Directions:

Ready... set... now preheat that oven!

**375° F**

*1.* In a mixing bowl, **mush** the butter and sugar together. Add in the egg, vanilla, buttermilk, water, flour, cocoa, baking powder, baking soda, and salt. **Whirl** until all of the ingredients have **mingled** into a dough.

*2.* Drop the dough, with an ice cream scoop, onto a parchment lined baking sheet, about 2 inches apart. Then, with the back of a kitchen spoon, smooth the top of each cookie.

*3.* Carefully place the baking sheet in the oven and bake away.

**9-10 minutes**

*4.* When the time is up, cautiously remove the baking sheet from the oven and allow the cookies to sit on the baking sheet, placed on a heat proof surface, to cool for 5 minutes. After the 5 minutes is up remove the cookies from the baking sheet with a metal spatula and place them on a wire rack to cool off further.

*5.* For the filling, in a large mixing bowl, **mush** the butter, vanilla and fluff together. Slowly add in the confectioners' sugar. Then, add the food coloring and crushed candy canes.

*6.* Once the cookies have cooled, take one cookie and spread a heaping tablespoon of filling on the flat side of the cookie. Then, top that filling with the flat side of another cookie.

## United States of America

# Red Velvet Whoopie Pies

## Directions:

**375° F**

Ready... set... now preheat that oven!

**1.** In a mixing bowl, **mush** the butter and sugar together. Add in the egg, vanilla, buttermilk, food coloring, water, flour, cocoa, baking powder, baking soda, and salt. **Whirl** until all of the ingredients have **mingled** into a dough.

**2.** Drop the dough, with an ice cream scoop, onto a parchment lined baking sheet, about 2 inches apart. Then, with the back of a kitchen spoon, smooth the top of each cookie.

**3.** Carefully place the baking sheet in the oven and bake away.

**9-10 minutes**

**4.** When the time is up, cautiously remove the baking sheet from the oven and allow the cookies to sit on the baking sheet, placed on a heat proof surface, to cool for 5 minutes. After the 5 minutes is up remove the cookies from the baking sheet with a metal spatula and place them on a wire rack to cool off further.

**5.** For the filling, in a large mixing bowl, **mush** the butter and cream cheese together. Slowly add in the confectioners' sugar and vanilla.

**6.** Once the cookies have cooled, take one cookie and spread a heaping tablespoon of filling on the flat side of the cookie. Then, top that filling with the flat side of another cookie.

## Ingredients:

3/4 cup butter, softened
1 cup sugar
1 egg
1 teaspoon vanilla extract
3/4 cup buttermilk
1 tablespoon red food coloring
2 1/4 cups all-purpose flour
1/4 cup dutch-processed
    cocoa powder
1/2 teaspoon baking powder
1/2 teaspoon baking soda
1/4 teaspoon salt

**For the filling:**
1/2 cup butter, softened
1 (8 oz.) package cream cheese
3 cups confectioners' sugar
1 teaspoon vanilla extract

## What you'll need:

measuring cups
measuring spoons
mixer with beater & bowl
large mixing bowl
ice cream scoop
parchment paper
baking sheet
metal spatula
wire cooling rack
kitchen spoon

## United States of America

# Spitzbuben

## Ingredients:

2 cups sugar
1 vanilla bean, rinsed and dried
1 1/8 cups butter
1 cup confectioners' sugar
2 teaspoons vanilla sugar
1/8 teaspoon salt
1 egg white
3 1/8 cups all-purpose flour
1 cup fruit preserves, any flavor
1/3 cup confectioners' sugar

## What you'll need:

measuring cups
measuring spoons
mason jar
mixer with beater & bowl
plastic wrap
baking sheet
metal spatula
wire cooling rack
kitchen spoon

## Directions:

375° F

Ready... set... now preheat that oven!

*1.* Three days prior to making these cookies you'll want to prepare some vanilla sugar: in a mason jar combine 2 cups of sugar and a vanilla bean. Cover and shake occasionaly.

*2.* In a mixing bowl, **mush** the butter and sugars together. Add in the flour and **whirl** until all of the ingredients have **mingled**.

*3.* Remove the mixing bowl from the mixer and cover the top of the bowl with plastic wrap. After covered, place the bowl in the **fridge** for 1 hour.

*4.* Remove the dough from the **fridge** and roll the dough out to 3/4 inch, on a floured surface. Then, with cookie cutters cut out large shapes, with smaller shapes cut out of the centers of half of the cut out cookies. Place the cut outs on a greased baking sheet.

*5.* Carefully place the baking sheet in the oven and bake away.

7-9 minutes

*6.* When the time is up, cautiously remove the baking sheet from the oven and allow the cookies to sit on the baking sheet, placed on a heat proof surface, to cool for 5 minutes. After the 5 minutes is up remove the cookies from the baking sheet with a metal spatula and place them on a wire rack to cool off further.

*7.* To assemble, spread your favorite preserve on the flat side of all of the cookies without a hole, then place the flat side of the cookies with a hole on top. Dust each cookie with confectioners' sugar.

# Tuiles

## Directions:

Ready... set... now preheat that oven!

375° F

*1.* In a mixing bowl, **mush** the butter and sugar together. Add in the egg whites, flour, almonds and vanilla. **Whirl** until all of the ingredients have **mingled**.

*2.* Using an ice cream scoop, **plop** two **blobs** of dough on a greased baking sheet and spread the dough into thin round shapes. Then carefully place the baking sheet in the oven and bake away.

8-10 minutes

*3.* When the time is up, cautiously remove the baking sheet from the oven and allow the cookies to sit on the baking sheet, placed on a heat proof surface, to cool for 1 minute. After the minute is up remove each cookie from the baking sheet with a metal spatula and place each cookie on a piece of wax paper, draped over a rolling pin. Let the cookies harden and cool.

*4.* Repeat until all of the dough has been baked and shaped.

## Ingredients:

4 tablespoons butter, softened
2/3 cup sugar
2 egg whites
4 tablespoons all-purpose flour
1 cup almonds, finely ground
1/4 teaspoon vanilla extract

## What you'll need:

measuring cups
measuring spoons
mixer with beater & bowl
baking sheet
wax paper
rolling pin
metal spatula
wire cooling rack

France

# Extra

# Chocolate Fudge

## Directions:

***1.*** In a large saucepan, **mingle** the marshmallow creme, sugar, evaporated milk, butter and salt together over medium heat.

***2.*** Bring the mixture to a full boil and continue to cook for an additional 5 minutes, stirring constantly.

***3.*** Remove the saucepan from the heat and add in all of the chocolate chips. Stir until all of the chocolate has melted. Once melted, add in the nuts (optional) and vanilla.

***4.*** Pour the mixture into an 8x8 pan, that has been lined with wax paper, and place in the **fridge** until firm.

## Ingredients:

1 (7 oz.) jar marshmallow fluff
1 1/2 cups sugar
2/3 cup evaporated milk
1/4 cup butter
1/4 teaspoon salt
2 cups milk chocolate chips
1 cup semisweet chocolate chips
1/2 cup walnuts, chopped (optional)
1 teaspoon vanilla extract

## What you'll need:

measuring cups
measuring spoons
large saucepan
8x8 baking pan
wax paper

# Your Family Favorites

Preheat oven to:   Bake for: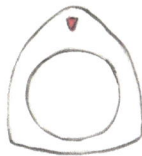

## Directions:

## Ingredients:

## What you'll need:

Preheat oven to: 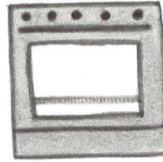    Bake for: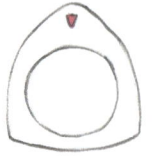

## Ingredients:

## Directions:

## What you'll need:

Preheat oven to: 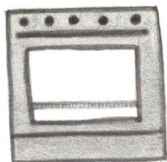　　Bake for:

## Directions:

## Ingredients:

## What you'll need:

Preheat oven to: 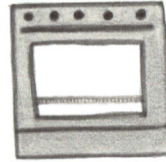   Bake for: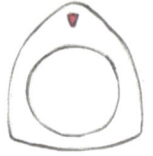

## Ingredients:

## Directions:

## What you'll need:

# About The Author

Lisa Oakman lives
(and eats a lot of cookies)
in upstate New York.

You can learn more about her and
her writing & illustration projects
by visiting her website at
www.lisaoakman.com .

# C🍪🍪kie Index

www.ingramcontent.com/pod-product-compliance
Lightning Source LLC
Chambersburg PA
CBHW061046090426

42740CB00002B/59

* 9 7 8 0 6 1 5 5 9 7 0 7 2 *